AF606955

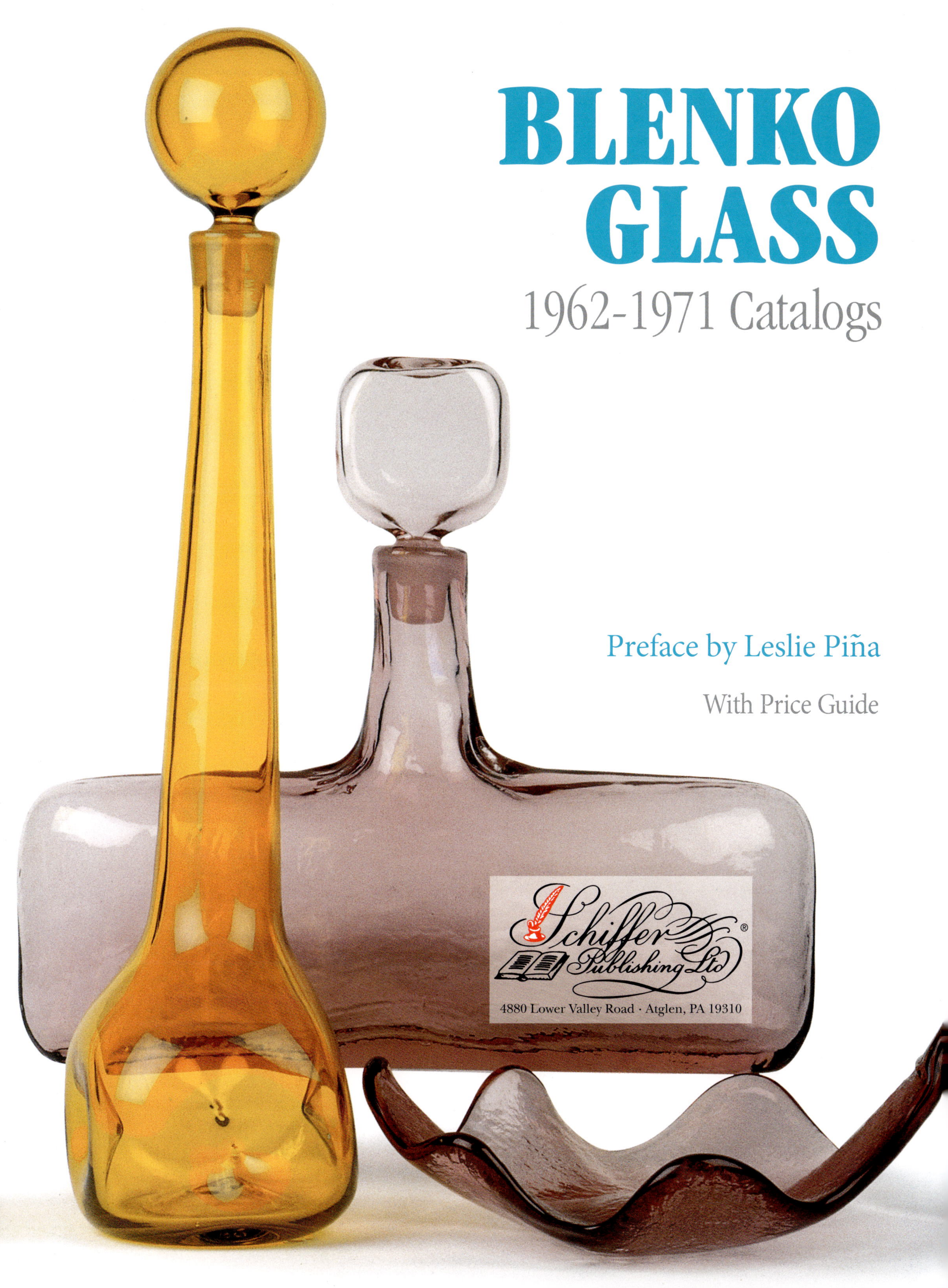

BLENKO GLASS
1962-1971 Catalogs
Preface by Leslie Piña
With Price Guide
Schiffer Publishing Ltd
4880 Lower Valley Road · Atglen, PA 19310

Acknowledgments

Many thanks to company president and friend Richard Deakin Blenko for making both Blenko projects possible. You can meet him at the Blenko Visitors Center and watch the glass blowers work at the adjoining factory in Milton. If you do, I hope that you enjoy your visit as much as I enjoyed mine.

Library of Congress Catalog Card Number: 99-66078

Designed by Leslie Piña
Layout by Bonnie M. Hensely
Type set in ZapfHumnst Dm BT/Korinna BT

ISBN: 978-0-7643-1026-3
Printed in China

Published by Schiffer Publishing Ltd.
4880 Lower Valley Road
Atglen, PA 19310
Phone: (610) 593-1777; Fax: (610) 593-2002
E-mail: Schifferbk@aol.com
Please visit our website catalog at
www.schifferbooks.com

This book may be purchased from the publisher.
Please try your bookstore first.
We are interested in hearing from authors
with book ideas on related subjects.
You may write for a free printed catalog.

Contents

Preface

by Leslie Piña

Blenko is one of the few remaining glass factories in the United States making modern hand blown production glass. Its history begins in the late nineteenth century when William Blenko left his native England to make stained glass in America. After several false starts, he built a tiny factory on the Mud River in Milton, West Virginia. To learn more about the story of Blenko's beginnings, I recommend two excellent resources, a book by Eason Eige and Rick Wilson (1987) and more recently a video by Witek & Novak (1998). Both sources carefully record and well-illustrate the early years of stained glass making, Colonial Williamsburg reproductions, and colorful tableware. They bring the audience up to the time of Blenko's first resident designer, Winslow Anderson, who worked at the factory from 1947 to 1952.

Recently, collectors have been focusing on the company's "middle" years of production, and in addition to Anderson's work, they have been scooping up Blenko designs from the 1950s and 1960s. Two other outstanding designers responsible for the entire design repertoire of that era were Wayne Husted and Joel Myers. Husted stayed from April of 1952 until January of 1963, after designing the 1963 line. (Numbers beginning with 53 through 63 are by Husted.) Myers began in January of 1963 and stayed until 1972.

The first all color company catalog was produced in 1959, with photography and graphics by Husted (creator of the next four catalogs as well). The following reprints, mostly from the Blenko archives, and also courtesy of Wayne Husted and the Huntington Museum of Art, are from the years 1962 to 1971—a very good decade. They are reprinted in their entirety, with the exception of duplicate pages of Williamsburg reproductions and some of the molded ashtrays. If a page seems to be missing from one catalog, it has already been shown in at least one other year. Each of the approximately 600 standard items produced during this very collectible period is pictured at least once. In order to retain an air of authenticity and historic integrity, handwritten notes have not been removed from any pages. After all, these were Blenko's personal catalogs that were used through the years.

Since designs were often carried for several years, many of Husted's '50s designs and some of Anderson's early designs are still shown in these catalogs along with most of Myer's work. The item number identifies the date and the design order. For example, 6513 is the thirteenth design for 1965. (The exception occurred in the early 1950s when Blenko used a 90 number instead of the year.) In this way, a numbered item can always be identified, even if out of context. If an early design is made at a later date, the color can often narrow the possibilities or even accurately date the item. For example, Rosé was produced only in 1963 and 1964.

I've included a price guide for each catalog item, which will prove most useful for the glass collectors and dealers referencing this book. Unfortunately, prices for Blenko glass widely vary and are apt to change quickly. On-line auctions have contributed to the dynamic marketplace, and this book along with any other reference should be used primarily to gather a range for an item's current selling price and to help readers distinguish between common, rare, and very desirable items. Since this is just a guide, you can expect to find any of the pieces at prices outside the range. All items are assumed to be in perfect condition with no nicks, scrapes, or water stains—condition is critical when assigning a value. Other features, such as color, also contribute to an item's price, i.e., Rosé will command a premium. Tangerine and other rich colors like red and cobalt are likewise very desirable, while colors like olive green, wheat, and crystal are usually found at the low end of the price range. Still, it is the shape and size that give each piece its "personality" and value.

This collection of catalog reprints should serve as a reference now and as a companion volume to the forthcoming book on Blenko glass. *Neither the author nor the publisher are responsible for any outcomes from consulting this price guide.* We do, however, wish you luck and fun in the search for Blenko and hope that this book will serve to that end.

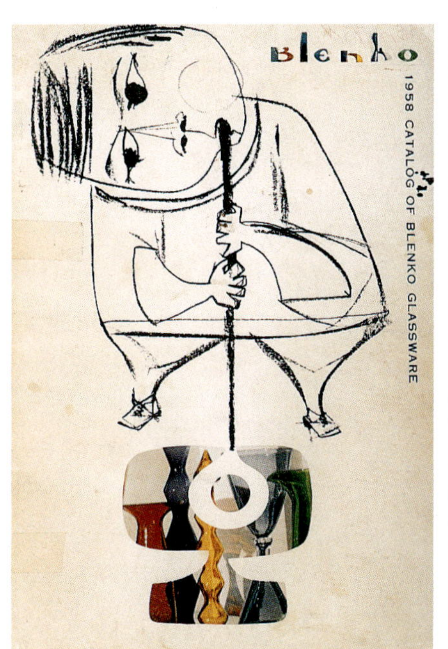

Blenko
1959 CATALOGUE OF HANDBLOWN GLASSWARE

1960
Blenko

14
Antique Green
Teardrop
CW-15 7½" high $5.00
CW-30 5½" high $4.50
CW-31L 4" high $54.00 doz.
CW-31S 3½" high $54.00 doz.
CW-34 3¾" high $48.00 doz.
CW-40 8½" high $8.00
CW-2W 6½" high $7.00
CW-2G 8" high $7.00
CW-2P 7¾" high $7.00
CW-2V 10" high $9.00
CW-2VL 12" high $12.00
Amber
CW-42-L 17¾" high $25.00
CW-42-S 11" high $15.00
CW-12 9½" high $4.50
CW-36-S 3¾" high $4.50
CW-38-P 7¾" high $10.00
CW-36-L 5" high $5.00
CW-14 6½" high $5.00
WILLIAMSBURG® ITEMS AVAILABLE AS FOLLOWS:
ALL STEMWARE MADE IN CRYSTAL ONLY.
These items available in Crystal only:
CW-6 CW-34 CW-42S
CW-14 CW-41 CW-42L
These items available in Crystal and Amethyst only:
CW-9 CW-10
CW-12 not available in Crystal, made in Amber, Emerald, Amethyst, and Sapphire
CW-40 not available in Crystal, made in Antique Green, Amber, Emerald, Amethyst, and Sapphire

15
Sapphire
CW-4 (Muddler) $1.00 Ea.
Balaster
CW-41 9" high $12.00
CW-5T 6" high $36.00 doz.
CW-5W 5¼" high $36.00 doz.
CW-5M 4¼" high $36.00 doz.
CW-5S 3" high $24.00 doz.
CW-1G 8" high $7.00
CW-1W 6½" high $7.00
CW-1S 5¼" high $7.00
CW-13 11¾" high $8.00
Amethyst
Airtwist
Emerald
CW-3G 8" high $8.50
CW-3W 6½" high $8.50
CW-3S 5⅞" high $8.50
CW-2S 5⅛" high $7.00
CW-6 7" high $9.00
CW-7 4¼" high $4.50 Ea.
CW-9 4¾" base dia. $12.00
CW-10 17½" high 5" base dia. $15.00
THESE ITEMS AVAILABLE IN CRYSTAL, EMERALD, AMETHYST, AND SAPPHIRE:
CW-4 (Muddler) CW-15
CW-5M CW-30
CW-5S CW-31S
CW-5T CW-31L
CW-5W CW-36-S
CW-7 CW-36-L
CW-13 CW-38P

1962

4
CHARCOAL
6217
21 ½" high
$7.50
6215
19" high
$7.50
6214
11" high
$6.00
6229
19" high
$7.00
6216
18 ¼" high
$7.50
6218
22 ¼" high
$10.00
6218
22 ¼" high
$10.00
CRYSTAL
6117
13⅞" high
$6.00
6220L
12 ¼" high
$6.00
6147
9 ¾" high
$8.00
6219L
9" high
$5.00
6219S
6⅞" high
$4.00
6221
12 ½" high
$6.00
6220S
10 ¾" high
$4.00
6226
15" high
$7.50

5

6228	*629	*37	*628S	*627L	*627S	*627S	603	6148
18" high	8⅛" high	13" high	24⅝"	18" high	12" high	12" high	7" high	11¼" high
$10.00	$7.00	$6.50	$9.00	$7.00	$4.50	$4.50	$4.00	$6.00

X

6212	*6030L	*6030M	*6030S	*6211	5825S	6037
20½" high	18½" high	13" high	10½" high	15¾" high	19½" high	21½" high
$9.00	$8.00	$6.50	$5.50	$9.00	$10.00	$11.00

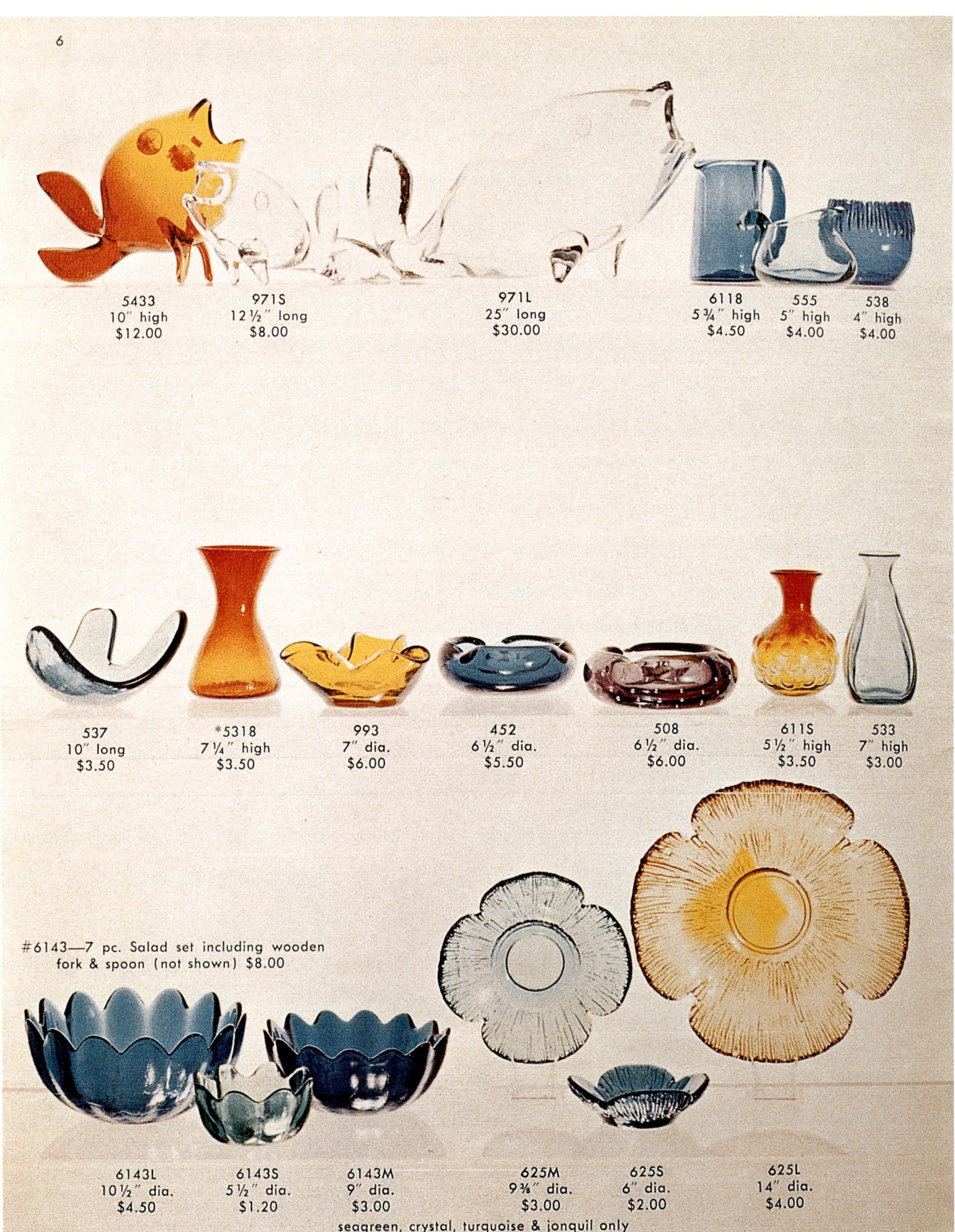
6

5433
10" high
$12.00

971S
12½" long
$8.00

971L
25" long
$30.00

6118
5¾" high
$4.50

555
5" high
$4.00

538
4" high
$4.00

537
10" long
$3.50

*5318
7¼" high
$3.50

993
7" dia.
$6.00

452
6½" dia.
$5.50

508
6½" dia.
$6.00

611S
5½" high
$3.50

533
7" high
$3.00

#6143—7 pc. Salad set including wooden fork & spoon (not shown) $8.00

6143L
10½" dia.
$4.50

6143S
5½" dia.
$1.20

6143M
9" dia.
$3.00

625M
9⅜" dia.
$3.00

625S
6" dia.
$2.00

625L
14" dia.
$4.00

seagreen, crystal, turquoise & jonquil only

7
*418L
6" high
$2.00
*418S
4 ½" high
$2.00
434
5 ½" high
(crystal only)
$6.00 pr.
C60A
4 ¾" high
$2.00
C60B
5" high
$2.00
C60F
3 ⅛" high
$2.00
C60C
4 ¾" high
$2.00
C60E
3 ⅜" dia.
$2.00
C60D
5 ¼" high
$2.00
6128
3 ½" long
$1.00
Miniatures not available in crystal
6023
7" dia.
$2.00
6023
7" dia.
$2.00
472
$1.50 box
59
(mixed colors only)
$1.00 box
966
8" long
$2.00
624
9 ⅜" dia.
$3.00
624
9 ⅜" dia.
$3.00
seagreen, crystal, turquoise & jonquil only
6139
6 ¼" dia.
$2.00
all colors
6112S
10" dia.
$3.00
6112L
12" dia.
$5.00
seagreen, crystal, turquoise & jonquil only

8
6113
14" high
$10.00
*388
7½" high
$5.50
*3716
11" dia.
$4.50
*3744X
7" diameter
$3.50
*622M
7⅜" high
$6.00
*622S
5⅝" high
$5.00
*622L
11½" high
$7.50
990A
3⅛" dia.
$1.00
*990
13¾" high
$6.50
*404M
11½" high
$7.00
*404S
9" high
$5.00
607
10" high
$3.50
964L
22" long
$12.00
964S
18½" long
$10.00
6026
10" high
$6.00
*3750L
5½" high
$4.50
*361P
7½" high
$6.00

9
51L
6" dia. bubbles
(in bowl)
$18.00 dz.
51
3" dia. bubbles
(in bowl)
$9.00 dz.
*920L
21 ¾" high
$9.00
*920S
10 ½" high
$5.00
*920
16 ½" high
$6.50
955L
17 ½" long
$7.50
*621M
10 ½" high
$4.00
*621S
9" high
$3.50
*621L
13 ¾" high
$5.00
*569P
13" high
$6.50
*626M
16 ¾" high
(not
shown)
$7.50
6120
12" high
$6.00
6042P
6 ¼" high
$5.00
6046
7 ½" high
$3.50
611S
5 ½" high
$3.50
6041
10 ½" high
$5.00
*6123S
11" high
$4.50
*6123M
13 ¼" high
$5.50
*626S
9⅞" high
$4.50
*6123L
21" high
$7.50
*626L
22" high
$12.00

10
*366L
12″ high
$6.50
*366M
9½″ high
$5.00
*6027
17″ high
$10.00
*49
10½″ high
$6.50
6110
13⅜″ high
$9.00
6115S
6¼″ high
$3.50
6115M
9⅝″ high
$4.50
6115L
14½″ high
$5.00
*546
10¾″ high
$6.50
5815M
24½″ high
$12.00
5815S
17″ high
$8.00
6230
18¾″ high
$7.50
619
8¾″ high
$6.00
6210
13⅞″ high
$7.50
*5519M
11¼″ high
$6.00
*5519L
16″ high
$7.50

11
6227
15" high
$6.00
6222
8 ¾" high
$3.50
6222
8 ¾" high
$3.50
6224S
7 ½" high
$5.00
6224S
7 ½" high
$5.00
6224L
10⅜" high
$7.00
6224L
10⅜" high
$7.00
6225L
21 ¼" high
$9.00
6225S
14⅝" high
$6.50
5616C
19 ¾" high
$6.00
5616B
15 ½" high
$5.00
*623L
10⅜" high
$7.00
*623S
8" high
$5.00
6223
12 ½" high
$4.00
6223
12 ½" high
$4.00
6213
22 ¾" high
$10.00
6213
22 ¾" high
$10.00

12
*6122L
26¾" high
$12.50
*6122S
16½" high
$7.00
*6122M
21½" high
$8.50
6141
6¾" high
$4.00
384
7½" high
$3.00
489
13" high
$15.00
413L
13" high
$9.00
*976
19½" high
$10.00
*366LL
12" high
$7.50
*366SL
7" high
$5.00
*366ML
9½" high
$6.00
6124
7" high
$5.00
991
13½" high
$7.50
*939P
14½" high
$7.00

13
628L
38 1/4" high
$15.00
6231
26 3/4" high
$15.00
6137
25 1/4" high
$15.00
5815L
31" high
$20.00
588
30" high
$17.50
5929L
38" high
$27.50
6138W/S
35 3/4" high
$17.50
(without stopper
$15.00)
*6029
27 1/2" high
$12.50
*6123LL
30" high
$12.00
5516W/S
32" high
$25.00
(without stopper
$22.50)
TURQUOISE
AMETHYST
TANGERINE
SEA GREEN
JONQUIL

1963

MAGNIFICENT COLOR, SKILLED CRAFTSMANSHIP AND CREATIVE DESIGN MAKE BLENKO AMERICA'S MOST COLORFUL NAME IN GLASS. EACH PIECE OF BLENKO IS AVAILABLE IN SIX COLORS. ALL BLENKO IS MADE OFF-HAND BY SKILLED ARTISANS WHO SPEND MANY YEARS LEARNING THE SKILLS OF GLASS BLOWING. NEW DESIGNS ARE ALWAYS IN PROGRESS AT BLENKO, MAKING THIS THE MOST TIMELY GLASS DESIGN IN AMERICA. THESE DESIGNS ARE UNIQUELY BLENKO.

BLENKO HANDCRAFT

BLENKO HANDCRAFT

4
6218
22 ¼″ high
$10.00
6217
21 ½″ high
$7.50
*636S
8″ high
$4.50
*636L
11″ high
$6.50
6223
12 ½″ high
$4.00
635 assorted
7″ diameter $2.50 ea.
6″ diameter $2.50 ea.
7″ x 4″ $2.50 ea.
6212L
28″ high
$15.00
6212
20 ½″ high
$9.00
*6212S
16″ high
$7.00
6210
13 ⅞″ high
$7.50
6215
19″ high
$7.50
639
14″ high
$6.00
6310
14″ high
$7.50

5
634
10″ dia.
$4.00
634
10″ dia.
$4.00
633
14″ long
$4.00
6322
6 ¼″ dia.
$3.50
*6311S
12″ high
$5.00
*6311M
15″ high
$6.50
*6311L
21 ¾″ high
$9.00
*637L
8 ½″ high
$6.50
*637M
7 ½″ high
$5.50
*637S
4 ¾″ high
$4.50
6316
12″ high
$15.00
6315
15 ¾″ high
$13.00
6314
21″ high
$12.00

6
*6030L
18 ½" high
$8.00
*6030M
13" high
$6.50
*6030S
10 ½" high
$5.50
*6027
17" high
$10.00
6222
8 ¾" high
$3.50
6222
8 ¾" high
$3.50
6226
15" high
$7.50
6227
15" high
$6.00
6225L
21 ¼" high
$9.00
6225S
15 ⅝" high
$6.50
6224S
7 ½" high
$5.00
6224S
7 ½" high
$5.00
6224L
10 ⅜" high
$7.00
6219S
6 ⅞" high
$4.00
6219L
9" high
$5.00
6220S
10 ¾" high
$4.00
6221
12 ½" high
$6.00

7
*976
19 ½" high
$10.00
991
13 ½" high
$7.50
*37
13" high
$6.50
6214
11" high
$6.00
6214
11" high
$6.00
*628S
24 ⅝" high
$9.00
*49
10 ½" high
$6.50
*627S
12" high
$4.50
*627L
18" high
$7.00
629L
10 ½" high
$11.00
629
8 ⅛" high
$7.00
*629S
6" high
$5.00
*6122M
21 ½" high
$8.50
*6122S
16 ½" high
$7.00
*6122L
26 ¾" high
$12.50

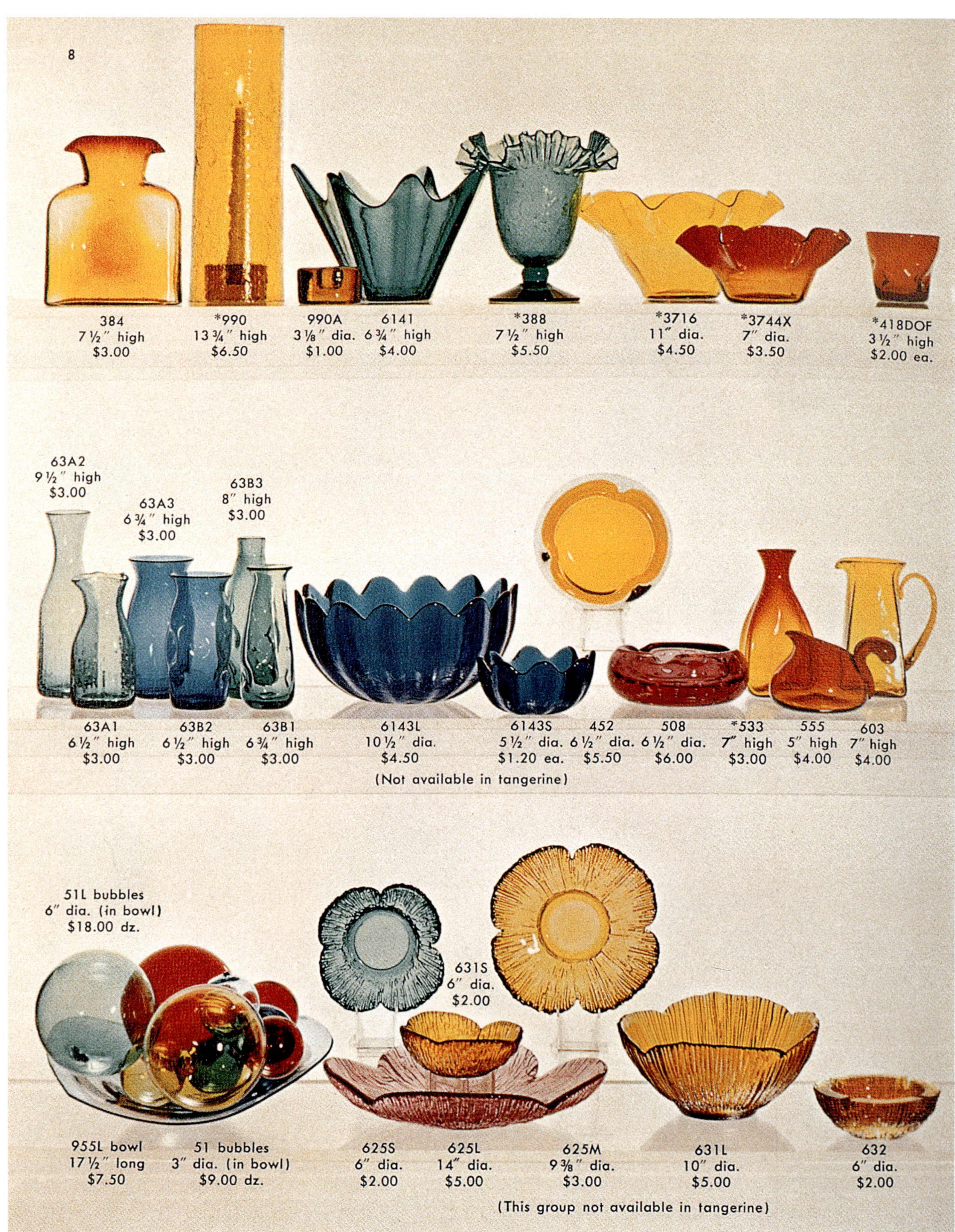
8
384
7 ½″ high
$3.00
*990
13 ¾″ high
$6.50
990A
3 ⅛″ dia.
$1.00
6141
6 ¾″ high
$4.00
*388
7 ½″ high
$5.50
*3716
11″ dia.
$4.50
*3744X
7″ dia.
$3.50
*418DOF
3 ½″ high
$2.00 ea.
63A2
9 ½″ high
$3.00
63A3
6 ¾″ high
$3.00
63B3
8″ high
$3.00
63A1
6 ½″ high
$3.00
63B2
6 ½″ high
$3.00
63B1
6 ¾″ high
$3.00
6143L
10 ½″ dia.
$4.50
6143S
5 ½″ dia.
$1.20 ea.
452
6 ½″ dia.
$5.50
508
6 ½″ dia.
$6.00
*533
7″ high
$3.00
555
5″ high
$4.00
603
7″ high
$4.00
(Not available in tangerine)
51L bubbles
6″ dia. (in bowl)
$18.00 dz.
631S
6″ dia.
$2.00
955L bowl
17 ½″ long
$7.50
51 bubbles
3″ dia. (in bowl)
$9.00 dz.
625S
6″ dia.
$2.00
625L
14″ dia.
$5.00
625M
9 ⅜″ dia.
$3.00
631L
10″ dia.
$5.00
632
6″ dia.
$2.00
(This group not available in tangerine)

9
*418L
6″ high
$2.00
*418S
4½″ high
$2.00
434
5½″ high
$6.00 pr.
C60A
4¾″ high
$2.00
C60B
5″ high
$2.00
C60F
3⅛″ high
$2.00
C60C
4¾″ high
$2.00
C60E
3⅝″ dia.
$2.00
C60D
5¼″ high
$2.00
6128
3½″ long
$1.00
Miniatures not available in crystal
6023
7″ dia.
$2.00
6023
7″ dia.
$2.00
472
$1.50 box
59
(mixed colors only)
$1.00 box
966
8″ long
$2.00
624
9⅜″ dia.
$3.00
624
9⅜″ dia.
$3.00
(Not available in tangerine)
6139
6¼″ dia.
$2.00
all colors
6112S
10″ dia.
$3.00
6112L
12″ dia.
$5.00
(Not available in tangerine)

10
*920L
21 ¾" high
$9.00
*920S
10 ½" high
$5.00
*920
16 ½" high
$6.50
*5519L
16" high
$7.50
*5519M
11 ¼" high
$6.00
413L
13" high
$9.00
384
7 ½" high
$3.00
*623L
10 ⅜" high
$7.00
*623S
8" high
$5.00
*6029
27 ½" high
$12.50
*569P
13" high
$6.50
*939P
14 ½" high
$7.00
*546
10 ¾" high
$6.50
*6211
15 ¾" high
$9.00
5616B
15 ½" high
$5.00
5616C
19 ¾" high
$6.00

11
*626L
22" high
$12.00
*626M
16 3/4" high
$7.50
*6123L
21" high
$7.50
*6123S
11" high
$4.50
*6123M
13 1/4" high
$5.50
*626S
9 7/8" high
$4.50
*3750L
5 1/2" high
$4.50
*638S
9 1/2" high
$5.00
*638M
15" high
$6.50
*638L
20" high
$9.00
5815M
24 1/2" high
$12.00
5815S
17" high
$8.00
*361P
7 1/2" high
$6.00
6115M
9 5/8" high
$4.50
6115S
6 1/4" high
$3.50
6115L
14 1/2" high
$5.00
6313S
7" high
$5.00
6313L
7 1/2" high
$6.00
6213
22 3/4" high
$10.00

12
*6323L
12½" high
$5.00
*6323S
6" high
$3.50
*6323M
9" high
$4.00
6317
7" high
$5.00
6321
4¼" dia.
$9.00 set
6320
3¼" dia.
$9.00 set
6319
5⅛" high
$6.00 pair
6318
6¼" high
$17.50 pair
5433
10" high
$12.00
964S
18½" long
$10.00
964L
22" long
$12.00
6312L
10" high
$7.00
6312M
7" high
$5.50
6312S
5" high
$4.50
6312S
5" high
$4.50
6326
4" dia.
$1.20 ea.
6326
4" dia.
$1.20 ea.
CRYSTAL
ROSÉ
971S
12½" long
$8.00
971L
25" long
$30.00
*366L
12" high
$6.50
*366M
9½" high
$5.00
*366LL
12" high
$7.50
*366ML
9½" high
$6.00
*366SL
7" high
$5.00
*404S
9" high
$5.00
*404M
11½" high
$7.00

13

*6123LL
30″ high
$12.00

627LL
32″ high
$12.50

5815L
31″ high
$20.00

6137
25 1/4″ high
$15.00

5929L
38″ high
$27.50

6138W/S
35 3/4″ high
$17.50

6138
(without stopper)
$15.00

6231
26 3/4″ high
$15.00

TANGERINE JONQUIL TURQUOISE SEA GREEN

14

CW-42-L
17¾" high
$25.00
Crystal Only

†CW-10
17½" high
5" base dia.
$15.00

†CW-9
4¾" base dia.
$11.00

CW-41
9" high
$12.00
Crystal Only

CW-40
8½" high
$7.50
Not made in Crystal

CW-12
9½" high
$4.50
Not Made in Crystal

CW-42-S
11" high
$15.00
Crystal Only

CW-38-P
7¾" high
$10.00

CW-36-L
5" high
$5.00

CW-36-S
3¾" high
$4.50

CW-6
7" high
$8.00
Crystal Only

CW-13
11¾" high
$8.00

CW-14
6½" high
$5.00
Crystal Only

"Williamsburg® Glass

Williamsburg® Glass Reproductions are handblown

WILLIAMSBURG Glass Reproductions are exact copies of originals in the famous exhibition buildings or are copies of fragments excavated in Williamsburg. These authentic reproductions are made exclusively by Blenko under a license granted by Williamsburg Restoration, Incorporated. This group of pieces is made in the jewel-like colors: amethyst, sapphire and emerald.

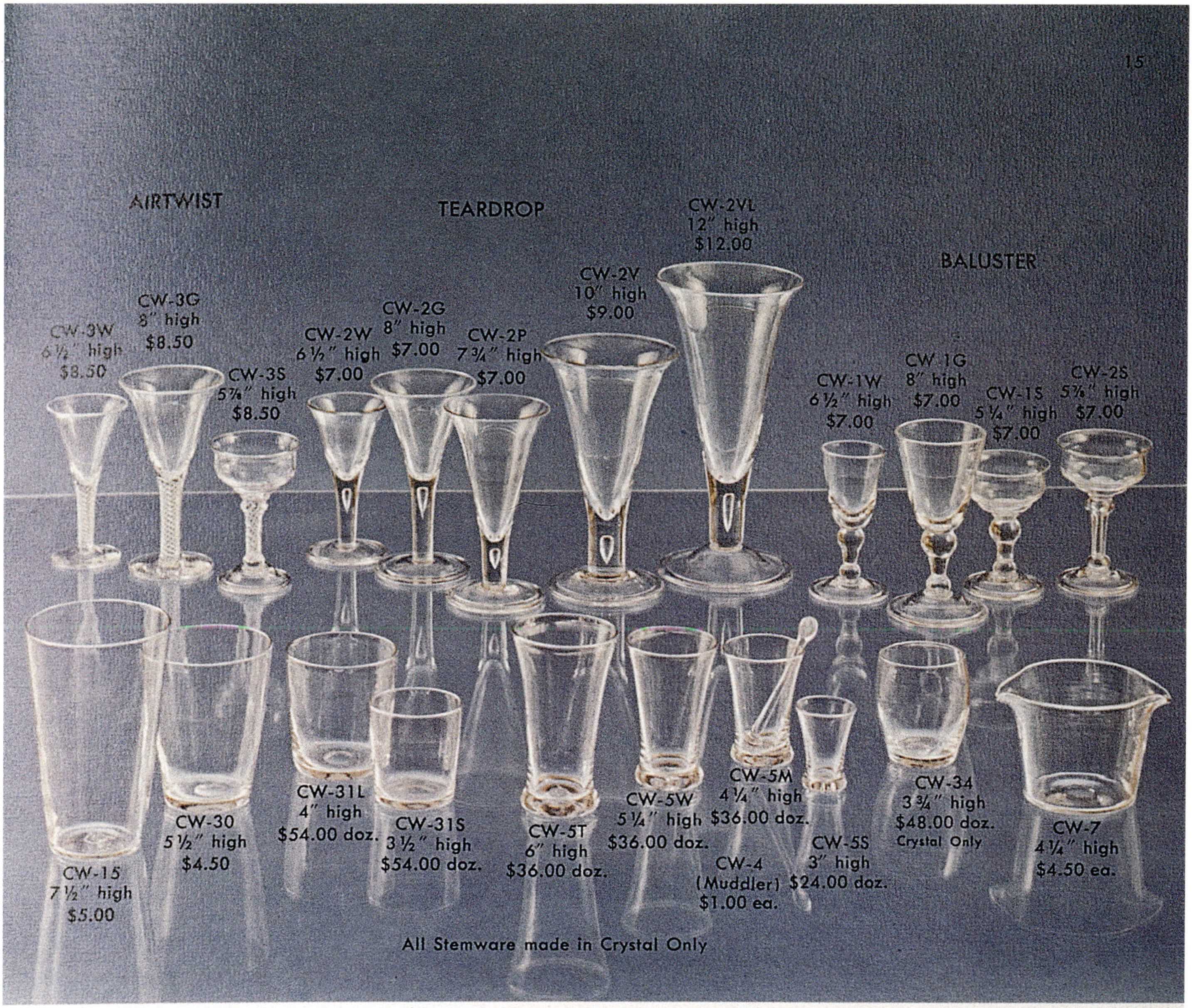

15

AIRTWIST

TEARDROP

BALUSTER

CW-3W 6½" high $8.50

CW-3G 8" high $8.50

CW-3S 5⅞" high $8.50

CW-2W 6½" high $7.00

CW-2G 8" high $7.00

CW-2P 7¾" high $7.00

CW-2V 10" high $9.00

CW-2VL 12" high $12.00

CW-1W 6½" high $7.00

CW 1G 8" high $7.00

CW-1S 5¼" high $7.00

CW-2S 5⅞" high $7.00

CW-15 7½" high $5.00

CW-30 5½" high $4.50

CW-31L 4" high $54.00 doz.

CW-31S 3½" high $54.00 doz.

CW-5T 6" high $36.00 doz.

CW-5W 5¼" high $36.00 doz.

CW-5M 4¼" high $36.00 doz.

CW-4 (Muddler) $1.00 ea.

CW-5S 3" high $24.00 doz.

CW-34 3¾" high $48.00 doz. Crystal Only

CW-7 4¼" high $4.50 ea.

All Stemware made in Crystal Only

Reproductions" by Blenko

by Blenko in especially pure ringing clear lead crystal glass.

WILLIAMSBURG and the hallmark (CW) are registered trade-marks of Williamsburg Restoration, Incorporated.

WILLIAMSBURG, VIRGINIA

Williamsburg items available as follows:
Crystal, Emerald, Amethyst, and Sapphire.
Crystal and amethyst only.
CW-12 and CW-40 are made in amber, emerald, amethyst and sapphire.

1964

BLENKO COLORS 1964

†NUMBERS PRECEDED BY A DAGGER ARE NOT AVAILABLE IN TANGERINE.
EACH PIECE IS AVAILABLE IN ALL SEVEN COLORS, UNLESS MARKED OTHERWISE.
*NUMBERS PRECEDED BY AN ASTERISK ARE AVAILABLE IN CRACKLED AS WELL AS PLAIN FINISH.

2
*6413
13¼" high
$7.00
*6414
9½" high
$7.50
6223
12½" high
$4.50
*3750L
5½" high
$4.50
*6122S
16½" high
$7.00
*6122M
21½" high
$8.50
6416
14⅛" high
$7.50
644
11" high
$5.00
*6412
8¼" high
$6.50
6417
16" high
$9.50
*6123M
13¼" high
$5.50
*6123L
21" high
$7.50

3

°990	990A	6411	°49	648	647
13¾″ high	3⅛″ dia.	3½″ dia.	10½″ high	15¼″ high	17¾″ high
$6.50	$1.00	$3.50	$6.50	$10.00	$9.00

°638L	°638M	°638S	6419	†633	°6422
20″ high	15″ high	9½″ high	9¾″ high	14″ long	16¾″ high
$9.00	$6.50	$5.00	$8.00	$4.00	$7.50

4
*627L
18" high
$7.00
*627S
12" high
$4.50
555
5" high
$4.00
*6027
17" high
$10.00
629
8⅛" high
$7.00
*629S
6" high
$5.00
629L
10½" high
$11.00
†631S
6" dia.
$2.00
*388
7½" high
$5.50
†625L
14" dia.
$5.00
*418L
6" high
$2.00
*418S
4½" high
$2.00
*418DOF
4" high
$2.50
*6311M
15" high
$6.50
*6311L
21¾" high
$9.00

5
†624
9⅜″ dia.
$3.00
6139
6¼″ dia.
$2.00
645
10″ high
$5.50
†632
6″ dia.
$2.00
646
17¼″ high
$7.00
†643
8″ dia.
$4.00
6023
7″ dia.
$2.00
6215
19″ high
$7.50
†641L
12″ dia.
$5.00
†6143S
5½″ dia.
$1.20 ea.
6420
11¾″ high
$7.50
964S
18½″ long
$10.00
964L
22″ long
$12.00
†6143L
10½″ dia
$4.50
6321
4¼″ dia.
$4.00 set
6320
3¼″ dia.
$5.00 set

6
51 bubbles (only)
3" dia.
$9.00 doz.
6115L
14½" high
$7.00
6115M
9⅝" high
$6.00
6115S
6¼" high
$5.00
955L
17½" long
$7.50
*637S
4¾" high
$4.50
*637M
7½" high
$5.50
*637L
8½" high
$6.50
†642S
8" dia.
$5.00
6423
18¼" high
$9.00
†642L
10" dia.
$7.00
†6128
3½" long
$1.00
†6428
11¼" dia.
$5.00
*366SL
7" high
$5.00
*366LL
12" high
$7.50
*366ML
9½" high
$6.00

51L bubbles (only)
6″ dia.
$18.00 doz.
WAR AND PEACE
Tolstoi
°649
13¼″ high
$7.00
384
7½″ high
$3.00
6418
22″ high
$10.00
966
8″ long
$2.00
°569P
13″ high
$6.50
434
5½″ high
$6.00 pair
°920L
21¾″ high
$9.00
°920
16½″ high
$6.50
°920S
10½″ high
$5.00
†641S
9¼″ dia.
$3.00
°404M
11½″ high
$7.50
°404S
9″ high
$5.50
991
13½″ high
$7.50

*64A
11¼″ high
$3.00
*64B
13″ high
$3.00
*64C
8″ high
$3.00
*976
19½″ high
$10.00
*623S
8″ high
$5.00
6313S
7″ high
$6.00
6218
22¼″ high
$10.00
6212L
28″ high
$15.00
6212
20½″ high
$9.00
*6212S
16″ high
$7.00
*628S
24⅝″ high
$9.00
*6424
5″ high
$2.50
*6029
27½″ high
$12.50

9
6213
22¾″ high
$10.00
*6030M
13″ high
$6.50
*6030L
18½″ high
$8.00
6310
14″ high
$7.50
6410
11½″ high
$6.00
5616C
approx. 22″ high
$6.00
*6425
27″ high
$7.50
*6427
25½″ high
$6.00
6322
6¼″ dia.
$3.50
6426
25¼″ high
$7.50
*6211
15¾″ high
$9.00
5815S
17″ high
$8.00
5815M
24½″ high
$12.00

10
*939P
14½" high
$7.00
59
(mixed colors only)
$1.00 box
472
$1.50 box
6421
16¼" high
$7.50
*636L
11" high
$7.00
*636S
8" high
$5.00
6415
21½" high
$7.50
6326
4" dia.
$1.20
†6319
5⅛" high
$6.00 pair
508
6½" dia.
$6.00
*366L
12"high
$7.00
452
6½" dia.
$5.50
*366M
9½" high
$5.50
603
7" high
$4.00
*37
13" high
$6.50
6225L
21¼" high
$9.00

11
°626L 22" high $12.00
°626M 16¾" high $7.50
°3744X 7" dia. $3.50
6224L 10⅜" high $7.00
6224S 7½" high $5.00
5433 10" high $12.00
639 14" high $7.00
6323L 12½" high $6.00
°6323M 9" high $5.00
°6323S 6" high $4.00
971M 16" long $15.00
971L 25" long $30.00
971S 12½" long $8.00
6217 21½" high $7.50

12
6138
without stopper
$15.00
6137
25¼" high
$15.00
5929L
38" high
$27.50
5815L
31" high
$20.00
°6123LL
30" high
$12.00
627LL
32" high
$12.50
6138 W/S
35¾" high
$17.50
6231
26¾" high
$15.00

BLENKO 1964—A FAMOUS NAME IN AMERICAN GLASSWARE

1965

BLENKO COLORS 1965

†NUMBERS PRECEDED BY A DAGGER ARE NOT AVAILABLE IN TANGERINE.
EACH PIECE IS AVAILABLE IN ALL SEVEN COLORS, UNLESS MARKED OTHERWISE.
*NUMBERS PRECEDED BY AN ASTERISK ARE AVAILABLE IN CRACKLED AS WELL AS PLAIN FINISH.
§ NUMBERS PRECEDED BY REFERENCE MARK ARE NOT AVAILABLE IN CHESTNUT AND PEACOCK OR TANGERINE.

2

*656L	*656M	*656S	*6517	*418S	*418L	*6526
14" high	10½" high	8½" high	10" high	4½" high	6" high	15¾" high
$8.00	$6.00	$5.00	$6.00	$2.00 ea.	$2.00 ea.	$9.00

*6211	*3744X	*657S	*657M	*657L	657LL
15¾" high	7" dia.	12" high	14" high	18½" high	22¾" high
$10.00	$3.50	$5.50	$7.50	$9.00	$11.50

3

645
10″ high
$5.50

646
17¼″ high
$7.00

*6424
5″ high
$3.00

6115M
9⅝″ high
$6.00

6115L
14½″ high
$7.00

6530S
14¼″ high
$6.50

6530L
16¾″ high
$8.50

*976
21¾″ high
$10.00

655
7½″ dia.
$4.00

*569P
13″ high
$6.50

†632
6″ dia.
$2.00

†624
9⅜″ dia.
$3.00

652
9″ high
$5.00 plus F.E.T.

6527
22¼″ high
$10.00

4
51 Bubbles (Only)
3" dia.
$9.00 doz.
*990
13¾" high
$7.00
§990A
3⅛" dia.
$1.00
6321
4¼" dia.
$4.00
6320
3¼" dia.
$5.00 plus F.E.T.
*629S
6" high
$6.00
*629
8⅛" high
$8.00
629L
10½" high
$12.00
§6128
3½" long
$1.00
§642L
10" dia.
$7.00
§642S
8" dia.
$5.00
*6422
16½" high
$7.50
6513
6" dia.
$7.50
6531
18¾" high
$12.50

5
*627L
18″ high
$7.00
*627S
12″ high
$5.00
§434
5½″ high
$6.00 pr.
647
17″ high
$10.00
648
19″ high
$11.00
6519
16½″ high
$14.00
6522
6½″ high
$4.00
6523
10¼″ high
$5.00
*6533
17¼″ high
$9.00
*654
11½″ high
$6.00
†643
8″ dia.
$4.00

6
51L Bubbles (Only)
6" dia.
$24.00 doz.
6520
18" high
$9.00
*6515
13½" high
$6.50
*388
7½" high
$6.00
955L
17½" long
$7.50
*366M
9½" high
$5.50
*366L
12" high
$7.00
†6143S
5½" dia.
$1.20 ea.
6529
20" high
$11.00
6521
14" high
$9.00
*636S
8" high
$5.00
*636L
11" high
$7.00
†6143L
10½" dia.
$4.50
*6311L
21¾" high
$9.00

7
6417
16" high
$9.50
*3750L
5½" high
$5.00
6525
13¼" high
$9.00
6410
11½" high
$6.00
6420
11¾" high
$7.50
6421
16" high
$7.50
†641S
9¼" dia.
$3.00
†631S
6" dia.
$2.00 ea.
6212
20½" high
$10.00
*6212S
16" high
$8.00
*6512
6" high
$5.00
*6516
14½" high
$6.00
†625L
14" dia.
$5.00
§6326
4" dia.
$1.20 ea.

8
6415
12½″ high
$7.50
†641L
12″ dia.
$5.00
*37
13″ high
$6.50
659L
16″ high
$8.00
659S
9¾″ high
$6.50
*649
13¼″ high
$7.00
6418
23″ high
$10.00
*920S
10½″ high
$5.00
*920
16½″ high
$6.50
*920L
23″ high
$9.00
†633
14″ long
$4.00
*6427
24″ high
$6.50
*6425
27″ high
$8.00

9
*6027
17″ high
$10.00
6224S
7½″ high
$5.00
6224L
10⅜″ high
$7.00
*6514
14¼″ high
$7.50
991
13½″ high
$7.50
6532
14½″ high
$10.00
5815M
23½″ high
$12.00
6416
14⅛″ high
$7.50
644
11″ high
$5.00 plus F.E.T.
*6524L
17″ high
$9.00
*6524S
13″ high
$7.00
*6528S
24″ high
$8.00
*6528L
31″ high
$10.00

10
64E
9″ high
$3.00
*64B
13″ high
$3.00
64D
11″ high
$3.00
*964L
22″ long
$13.00
§6319
5⅛″ high
$6.00 pr.
653
16½″ high
$5.00
*6510
12½″ high
$9.00
*6412
8¼″ high
$6.50
658S
16½″ high
$7.00
658L
21″ high
$9.00
472
$1.50 box
59
(mixed colors
only)
$1.00 box
6023
7″ dia.
$2.00
6518
12″ high
$7.00

971L
25" long
$30.00
971M
16" long
$15.00
971S
12½" long
$8.00
5433
10" high
$12.00
6139
6¼" dia.
$2.00
*49
10½" high
$6.50
*939P
14½" high
$7.00
*623S
8" high
$5.00
966 (assorted)
8" long
$2.00
6423
18½" high
$10.00
6511
9½" high
$5.00
B508
6½" dia.
$6.00
384
7½" high
$3.00

12
6138 without stopper $15.00
6534
29″ high
$20.00
5929L
38″ high
$27.50
5815L
31″ high
$20.00
6536
23½″ high
$15.00
6138W/S
35¾″ high
$17.50
6535
43″ high
$27.50

16
†65D
†65F
†65A
†65F
†65A
†65E
†65C
†65B
†65E
†65D
†65C
†65B
All numbers 65 are DECORATIVE DISCS with two holes for hanging, the letters indicate their respective designs. Approximate size 8¼" diameter. Price $3.50 each.
All numbers 651 are ASH TRAYS and use same code letters for designs as numbers 65. Approximate size 9" diameter. Price $4.00 each.
†651F
†651B
650 8" x 8" x 1" DECORATIVE SLABS Available in assorted Cathedral Glass Colors. $4.00 Each

1966

BLENKO COLORS 1966

†NUMBERS PRECEDED BY A DAGGER ARE NOT AVAILABLE IN TANGERINE.
EACH PIECE IS AVAILABLE IN ALL SIX COLORS, UNLESS MARKED OTHERWISE.
*NUMBERS PRECEDED BY AN ASTERISK ARE AVAILABLE IN CRACKLED AS WELL AS PLAIN FINISH.
§ NUMBERS PRECEDED BY REFERENCE MARK ARE NOT AVAILABLE IN PEACOCK OR TANGERINE.

2
6421
16" high
$8.00
6523
10¼" high
$6.00
6612
10¾" high
$4.00
6139
6¼" dia.
$2.00
6518
10½" high
$8.00
6519
16½" high
$15.00
6613
16⅝" high
$7.50
6628
12⅝" high
$8.00
6627
17⅛" high
$9.00
6622
10½" high
$7.00
6415
12½" high
$7.50

3

°6623
14⅛″ high
$7.00

†661
6½″ dia.
$2.00

†664
13¼″ dia.
$5.00

6027
17″ high
$10.00

6530S
14¼″ high
~~$7.00~~
7.50

6530L
16¾″ high
~~$8.50~~
9.00

6212
20½″ high
$10.00

°6424
5″ high
$3.00

°636S
8″ high
$5.00

658L
21″ high
$9.00

658S
16½″ high
~~$7.00~~
7.50

†633
14″ long
~~$4.00~~
5.00

4
6611
13″ high
$7.00
6616
7⅜″ high
$5.50
6610
9″ high
$4.50
6115L
14½″ high
$7.50
6115M
9⅝″ high
$6.00
B508
6½″ dia.
$6.00
6532
14½″ high
$11.00
*657L
18½″ high
$10.00
*657M
14″ high
$7.50
*657S
12″ high
$6.00
*656M
10½″ high
$6.50
*656S
8½″ high
$5.00
*6526
15¾″ high
$10.00

5
*3750L
5½″ high
$5.00
*388
7½″ high
$6.00
6.50
†662
6¾″ dia.
$2.00
†663
9⅝″ dia.
$5.00
*654
11½″ high
$7.00
*6533
17¼″ high
$10.00
6617
10¼″ high
$7.00
955L
17½″ long
$8.50
6634
19¾″ high
$10.00
64E
9″ high
$3.00
64D
11″ high
$3.00
*64B
13″ high
$3.00
653
16½″ high
$6.00

6
6615L
14″ high
$8.50
6615S
10⅞″ high
$7.00
*6614
5″ high
$4.50
*939P
14½″ high
$7.00
*3744X
7″ dia.
$3.50
†632
6″ dia.
$2.00
§434
5½″ high
$6.00 pr.
†6143S
5½″ dia.
$1.20
5815M
23½″ high
$12.00
†6143L
10½″ dia.
$4.50
*649
13¼″ high
$7.50
†666A
5½″ dia.
$1.50
*666B
4½″ high
$4.00
*37
13″ high
$7.00
384
7½″ high
$3.00

7
6416
14⅛" high
$7.50
°629
8⅛" high
$8.00
°629S
6" high
$6.00
6525
13¼" high
$9.00
669
8½" high
$6.00
§990A
3⅛" dia.
$1.00
°990
12" high
$7.00
°6626L
18½" high
$8.50
°6626S
15" high
$7.00
°667L
5⅞" high
$6.00
°667S
4¼" high
$4.50
°6528S
24" high
$8.00
°6524S
13" high
$7.50
†643
8" dia.
$4.00

8
*366L
12" high
$7.00
*366M
9½" high
$5.50
645
10" high
$5.50
646
17¼" high
$7.50
644
11" high
$5.00
6624S
4½" high
$8.00
6624L
8" high
$10.00
6631
21½" high
$10.00
966 (assorted)
8" long
$2.00
6511
9½" high
$5.00
*6427
24" high
$7.50
*6621
6⅜" high
$6.50
659S
9¾" high
$6.50
659L
16" high
$8.00

9
°6630L
13¾″ high
$8.00
°6630S
8⅞″ high
$6.00
6618
14″ high
$7.00
°6629
12⅝″ high
$8.00
°668S
6¼″ high
$5.00
°668L
7⅞″ high
$7.00
°627L
18″ high
$7.50
†624
9⅜″ dia.
$3.00
6632
16¼″ high
$10.00
6418
23″ high
$12.00

10
51L Bubbles only
6″ dia.
$24.00 dozen
°6512
6″ high
$5.50
°6516
14½″ high
$7.00
7.50
°964L
22″ long
$15.00
6224L
10⅜″ high
$7.50
6224S
7½″ high
$5.50
6625
7¾″ high
$10.00
6529
20″ high
$12.00
6513
6″ dia.
$7.50
6023
7″ dia.
$2.00
59
(mixed colors
only)
$1.00 box
472
$1.50 box
°6619
11″ high
$7.50
°6620
9½″ high
$6.00

11
51 Bubbles (only)
3″ dia.
$9.00 dozen
971L
25″ long
$30.00
971M
16″ long
$15.00
971S
12½″ long
$9.00
5433
10″ high
$12.00
*418L
6″ high
$2.00
*418S
4½″ high
$2.00
§665B
Approx. 6″ dia.
$2.00
6633
17¼″ high
$10.00
†641L
12″ dia.
$5.00
§665A
Approx. 6″ dia.
$2.00
§665C
Approx. 6″ dia.
$2.00
*49
10½″ high
$7.00
991
13½″ high
$7.50

16
†65E
†65H
†65G
†65B
†65F
†65J
†65F
†65E
†65B
†65F
†65H
†65F
†65G
†65E
All numbers 65 are DECORATIVE DISCS with two holes for hanging. The letters indicate their respective designs. Approximate size 8¼″ diameter. Price $3.50 each.
All numbers 651 are ASH TRAYS and use same code letters for designs as numbers 65. Approximate size 9″ diameter. Price $4.00 each.
CW-43L
5⁷⁄₁₆″ high
$4.50 ea.
CW-43S
5⁷⁄₁₆″ high
$4.50 ea.
†651J
†651F

12
6138 without stopper $15.00
6534
29″ high
$25.00
5929L
38″ high
$30.00
5815L
31″ high
$20.00
6536
23½″ high
$15.00
6138W/S
35¾″ high
$17.50
6535
43″ high
$30.00

1967

BLENKO COLORS 1967

† NUMBERS PRECEDED BY A DAGGER ARE NOT AVAILABLE IN TANGERINE.
EACH PIECE IS AVAILABLE IN ALL SIX COLORS, UNLESS MARKED OTHERWISE.
* NUMBERS PRECEDED BY AN ASTERISK ARE AVAILABLE IN CRACKLED AS WELL AS PLAIN FINISH.
§ NUMBERS PRECEDED BY REFERENCE MARK ARE NOT AVAILABLE IN PLUM OR TANGERINE.

4
°366L
12" high
$7.00
°366M
9½" high
$6.00
6530S
14¼" high
$7.50
6530L
16¾" high
$9.00
†624
9⅜" dia.
$3.00
644
11" high
$6.00
†6139
6¼" dia.
$2.00
6717
21" high
$10.00
6731
10¼" high
$5.00
6728
16¾" high
$7.50
6729
4⅜" high
$8.00
6730
4¾" high
$5.00
991
13½" high
$7.50
384
7½" high
$3.00

5
6711L
15½″ high
$10.00
6711S
11½″ high
$8.00
672
12″ dia.
$4.00
†632
6″ dia.
$2.00
*627L
18″ high
$7.50
6713
22¼″ high
$10.00
6712
11¼″ high
$8.00
†666A
5½″ dia.
$1.50
666B
4½″ high
$4.00
*37
13″ high
$7.50
6632
16¼″ high
$10.00
6418
23″ high
$12.00

6

678
10¼″ high
$6.00

677
9¼″ high
$4.50

679
7″ high
$5.00

6610
9″ high
$4.50

6718
3¾″ high
$5.00

6720
10¼″ high
$7.00

67S
13½″ high
4¾″ dia. base
$12.00
Plum and Crystal only

67L
17½″ high
5″ dia. base
$15.00
Crystal only

669
8½″ high
$6.00

6224S
7½″ high
$5.50

*636S
8″ high
$5.00

*6619
11″ high
$7.50

6719
14½″ dia.
$5.00

†664
13¼" dia.
$5.00
*6630S
8⅞" high
$6.00
*964L
22" long
$15.00
6511
9½" high
$5.00
6617
10¼" high
$7.00
6738
18½" high
$9.00
6737
14¼" high
$7.00
*3744X
7" dia.
$3.50
*6516
14½" high
$7.50
*6512
6" high
$5.50
5815M
23½" high
$12.00

8
§6725
3½" high
3¾" wide
$6.00 pr.
6612
10¾" high
$4.00
6727
13" high
$5.00
659S
9¾" high
$6.50
659L
16" high
$8.00
*388
7½" high
$6.50
59
Mixed Colors Only
$1.00 box
472
$1.50 box
6536
23½" high
$15.00
6739
28½" high
$10.00
6744
14½" high
$6.50
6743
21⅝" high
$8.00
6745
29" high
$12.50
6733
14¾" high
$5.50
6732S
19¼" high
$7.50
6732L
24¼" high
$10.00

9
*990
12" high
$7.00
§990A
3⅛" dia.
$1.00
§676
2½" high
$1.00
*3750L
5½" high
$5.00
†633
14" long
$5.00
64E
9" high
$3.00
64D
11" high
$3.00
*64B
13" high
$3.00
653
16½" high
$6.00
6736
22⅜" high
$12.50
*6427
24" high
$7.50
6741
23¼" high
$12.50
6740
15⅛" high
$9.00
6742
11¾" high
$8.00
6747
27¼" high
$15.00

10
6615L
14" high
$8.50
6615S
10⅞" high
$7.00
*6614
5" high
$5.00
*657M
14" high
$8.00
*656M
10½" high
$6.50
*656S
8½" high
$5.00
6027
17" high
$10.00
6627
17½" high
$9.00
6628
12⅝" high
$8.00
*6629
12⅝" high
$8.00
6715
(no plum)
15¾" high
$12.00
6710B
turquoise/olive only
9½" high
$9.00
6710A
tangerine/honey only
9½" high
$9.00
6746
21¾" high
$9.00

11
*629
8½″ high
$8.00
*629S
6″ high
$6.00
671
9½″ dia.
$3.00
674
6″ dia.
$2.00
*6714
8¾″ high
$6.50
*418S
4½″ high
$2.00
*418L
6″ high
$2.00
*6734
16¾″ high
$7.00
*667S
4¼″ high
$4.50
*667L
5⅞″ high
$6.00
675
(slotted ashtray)
9¾″ dia.
$3.50
6735
14¾″ high
(approx.)
$6.00
†6143S
5½″ dia.
$1.20
†6143L
10½″ dia.
$4.50

12
°939P
14½" high
$7.50
°6424
5" high
$3.00
6723
(no plum)
11½" high
$7.00
6724
(no plum)
14" high
$10.00
6716
14¼" high
$12.00
°6626S
15" high
$7.00
°6626L
18½" high
$8.50
6529
20" high
$12.00
966
(assorted)
8" long
$2.00
°6726
9⅛" high
$7.50
°6721L
16½" high
$10.00
°6721S
12¾" high
$8.00
6212
20½" high
$10.00

13
51 bubbles only
3" dia.
$9.00 dozen
971L
25" long
$30.00
971M
16" long
$15.00
971S
12½" long
$9.00
5433
10" high
$12.00
§673
8¾" dia.
$2.50
658S
16½" high
$7.50
6722
14" high
$6.50
6415
12½" high
$7.50
*49
10½" high
$7.00
646
17¼" high
$7.50
645
10" high
$5.50
6320
3¼" dia.
$5.50
6321
4¼" dia.
$4.50
6115L
14½" high
$7.50

14
51L
bubbles only
6" dia.
$24.00 dozen
6518
12" high
$8.00
955L
17½" long
$8.50
B508
(no plum)
6½" dia.
$6.00
6624S
4½" high
$9.00
6513
(no plum)
6" dia.
$7.50
6631
21½" high
$11.00
*668L
7⅞" high
$7.00
*668S
6¼" high
$5.00
*6528S
24" high
$8.00
6023
7" dia.
$2.00
§434
5½" high
$6.00 pr.

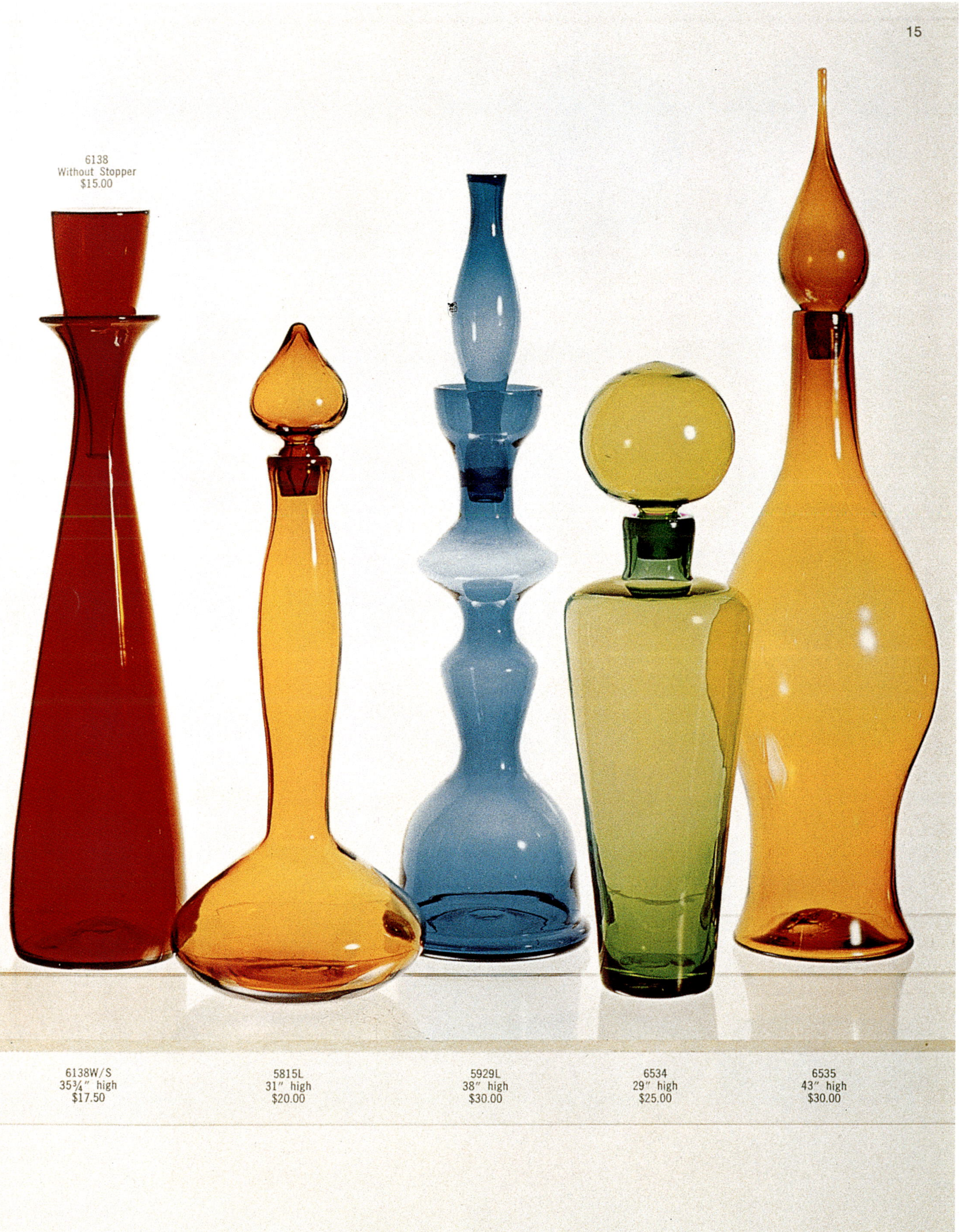
15
6138
Without Stopper
$15.00
6138W/S
35¾″ high
$17.50
5815L
31″ high
$20.00
5929L
38″ high
$30.00
6534
29″ high
$25.00
6535
43″ high
$30.00

1968

BLENKO COLORS 1968

† NUMBERS PRECEDED BY A DAGGER ARE NOT AVAILABLE IN TANGERINE.
EACH PIECE IS AVAILABLE IN ALL SIX COLORS, UNLESS MARKED OTHERWISE.
* NUMBERS PRECEDED BY AN ASTERISK ARE AVAILABLE IN CRACKLED AS WELL AS PLAIN FINISH.
§ NUMBERS PRECEDED BY A REFERENCE MARK ARE AVAILABLE IN COLOR SCHEMES ILLUSTRATED ON THE BOTTOM OF PAGE 9.

4

°629
8½″ high
$8.00

°629S
6″ high
$6.50

°366L
12″ high
$7.00

°366M
9½″ high
$6.00

6710B
9½″ high
turquoise/olive only
$9.00

6710A
9½″ high
tangerine/honey only
$9.00

6027
17″ high
$10.00

6741
crystal stoppers only
with Lemon or
Tangerine Bottles
23¼″ high
$13.50

6742
11¾″ high
$8.00

6740
15⅛″ high
$9.00

6320
3¼″ dia.
$5.50

6321
4¼″ dia.
$4.50

†666A
5½″ dia.
$1.50

666B
4½″ high
$4.00

644
11″ high
$6.00

67L
crystal only
17½″ high
5″ dia. base
$15.00

67S
crystal only
13½″ high
4¾″ dia. base
$12.00

*964L
22″ long
$15.00

*37
13″ high
$7.50

*388
7½″ high
$6.50

*3744X
7″ dia.
$3.50

*49
10½″ high
$7.00

6717
crystal stopper only
with Lemon or
Tangerine Bottle
21″ high
$11.00

†6813
7″ high
$6.00 pr.

†6725
3½″ high
3¾″ wide
$6.00 pr.

†434
5½″ high
$6.00 pr.

†683
6⅝″ dia.
$2.00 ea.

6631
21½″ high
$11.00

6
6819
13½″ high
$7.50
6812
9⅜″ high
$4.00
6820
11½″ high
$9.00
6829
12½″ high
$7.50
6827
9½″ high
$6.50
6828
6½″ high
$5.50
6842
16¼″ high
$10.00
Crystal only, with
Crystal, Turquoise,
Honey, & Olive Stoppers
No Tangerine or Lemon Stoppers
Trim available in all colors
for the above three items
6841
21″ high
$9.00
*6821
14″ high
$7.50
Crystal Only
with all colors except
Lemon or Tangerine as Trim
6823
14″ high
$9.00
*688
10″ high
$5.00
*689
5¾″ high
$5.00
*6839
14″ high
$6.50

7
†686
13½″ dia.
$6.00
†632
6″ dia.
$2.00
†685S
7½″ dia.
$1.20
†684
7⅜″ dia.
$2.00
†685L
12½″ dia.
$5.00
†675
slotted ashtray
9¾″ dia.
$3.50
†681
8⅛″ dia.
$2.50
†6139
6¼″ dia.
$2.00
†624
9⅜″ dia.
$3.00
†6143S
5½″ dia.
$1.20
†6143L
10½″ dia.
$4.50

§°6836-OT
13¾" high
$8.00

§°6843-TO
8½" high
$6.00

§°6830-OT
15½" dia.
Approx. 14" high
$25.00

§°6833-OT
10⅝" high
$4.00

§°6832-OT
12¾" high
$6.00

§°6837-LT
13⅛" high
$8.50

6811
16¼" high
$8.00

6810
10¾" high
$5.50

§6822-CH
18¼" high
$9.00

§6835-OT
17½" high
$10.00

§6831-CH
23" high
$10.00

§6834-OT
17½" high
$8.00

§°6815-OT
10" high
$5.00

§°6814-LT
10" high
$5.50

§°6816-TO
15½" high
$7.00

§°6817-CT
9" high
$4.00

§°6818-OT
9" high
$6.00

§°6840-TO
6" high
15½" dia.
$10.00

§°6838-TO
15¾" high
Turquoise with
Olive Trim
$7.50

§°6838-CT
15¾" high
Crystal with
Turquoise Trim
$7.50

§°6838-CH
15¾" high
Crystal with
Honey Trim
$7.50

§°6838-LT
15¾" high
Lemon with
Tangerine Trim
$7.50

§°6838-OT
15¾" high
Olive with
Turquoise Trim
$7.50

§°6838-CO
15¾" high
Crystal with
Olive Trim
$7.50

Numbers with a reference mark (§) are available in the above color combinations. The suffix code after the item number indicates a particular color combination. These combinations and their coding are as follows:

TO — turquoise with olive trim
CT — crystal with turquoise trim
CH — crystal with honey trim
LT — lemon with tangerine trim
OT — olive with turquoise trim
CO — crystal with olive trim

971L	971M	971S	5433	6733	6732S
25″ long	16″ long	12½″ long	10″ high	14¾″ high	19¼″ high
$30.00	$15.00	$9.00	$12.00	$5.50	$7.50

6418	6632	6224S	*636S	669	*6630S	*64B	*687	64D
23″ high	16¼″ high	7½″ high	8″ high	8½″ high	8⅞″ high	13″ high	8″ high	11″ high
$12.00	$10.00	$5.50	$5.50	$6.00	$6.00	$3.00	$3.00	$3.00

*6516 14½" high $7.50 | *6512 6" high $5.50 | *3750L 5½" high $5.00 | *668L 7⅞" high $7.00 | *668S 6¼" high $5.00 | 6511 9½" high $5.50

645 10" high $5.50 | *656S 8½" high $5.50 | 991 13½" high $7.50 | 384 7½" high $3.00 | *418S 4½" high $2.00 ea. | *418L 6" high $2.00 ea. | *6714 9¾" high $7.00

12
6716
14¼" high
$12.00
Crystal Stopper with
Lemon or Tangerine
Bottle
6513
6" dia.
$7.50
B508
6½" dia.
$6.00
*6424
5" high
$3.00
*6726
9⅛" high
$8.00
*6721S
12¾" high
$8.00
6722
14" high
$7.00
6415
12½" high
$7.50
*6427
24" high
$7.50
6115L
14½" high
$7.50
*990
12" high
$7.00
†990A
3⅛" dia.
$1.00 ea.
*6734
16¾" high
$7.50

13
51 Bubbles only
3" dia.
$9.00 dozen
51M Bubbles only
4½" dia.
$15.60 dozen
51L Bubbles only
6" dia.
$24.00 dozen
*633
14" long
$5.00
472
$1.50 box
59
Mixed Colors Only
$1.00 box
955L
17½" long
$8.50
*6614
5" high
$5.00
6711S
11½" high
$8.50
6736
22⅜" high
$15.00
Crystal Stopper only
with Lemon or
Tangerine Bottle
6212
20½" high
$10.00
*6629
12⅝" high
$8.50
6723
11½" high
$7.00
6724
14" high
$10.00
Crystal Stopper only
with Lemon or
Tangerine Bottle
6530S
14¼" high
$8.00
6624S
4½" high
$9.00

14
68C
Approx.
3¾″ dia.
$4.00
68A
Approx.
3¾″ dia.
$4.00
No Lemon
or Tangerine
68B
Approx.
3¾″ dia.
$4.00
No Lemon
or Tangerine
6824
Approx.
6¼″ high
$7.50 ea.
No Lemon
or Tangerine
6826B
Approx.
4″ high
$8.00
No Lemon
or Tangerine
6826A
Approx.
4″ high
$7.00
No Lemon
or Tangerine
6825
Approx.
6½″ dia.
$7.00 ea.
No Lemon
or Tangerine
†682
7¼″ dia.
$2.50
6745
29″ high
$12.50
Crystal Stopper only
with Lemon or
Tangerine Bottles
6744
14½″ high
$6.50
°6528S
24″ high
$9.00
†966
(assorted)
8″ long
$2.00
†6023
7″ dia.
$2.00
6739
28½″ high
$12.00
6735
Approx.
14¾″ high
$6.00

15
6138
Without Stopper
$15.00
6535
43″ high
$30.00
5815L
31″ high
$20.00
6534
29″ high
$25.00
6138W/S
35¾″ high
$17.50

16

†65J
8¼" dia.
$3.50

†65E
8¼" dia.
$3.50

†65B
8¼" dia.
$3.50

†65L
8¼" dia.
$3.50

†65F
8¼" dia.
$3.50

†65B
8¼" dia.
$3.50

†65K
8¼" dia.
$3.50

†65J
8¼" dia.
$3.50

†632
6" dia.
$2.00

†682
7¼" dia.
$2.50

6321
4¼" dia.
$4.50

6826A
Approx.
4" high
$7.00
No Lemon
or Tangerine

†666A
5½" dia.
$1.50

†681
8⅛" dia.
$2.50

†624
9⅜" dia.
$3.00

†675
slotted ashtray
9¾" dia.
$3.50

†651F
9" dia.
$4.00

†684
7⅜" dia.
$2.00

B508
6½" dia.
$6.00

†6139
6¼" dia.
$2.00

6513
6" dia.
$7.50

†6023
7" dia.
$2.00

†966
(assorted)
8" long
$2.00

BLENKO 1968 BLENKO 1968 BLENKO 1968

1969

LEMON TURQUOISE CRYSTAL TANGERINE OLIVE GREEN WHEAT

BLENKO COLORS 1969

† NUMBERS PRECEDED BY A DAGGER ARE NOT AVAILABLE IN TANGERINE.
EACH PIECE IS AVAILABLE IN ALL SIX COLORS, UNLESS MARKED OTHERWISE.
* NUMBERS PRECEDED BY AN ASTERISK ARE AVAILABLE IN CRACKLED AS WELL AS PLAIN FINISH.
§ NUMBERS PRECEDED BY A REFERENCE MARK ARE AVAILABLE IN COLOR SCHEMES ILLUSTRATED ON THE TOP OF PAGE 12.

4

18.00

13.50

67L
17½" high
7" dia. base
~~$17.00~~

67S
15" high
6¾" dia. base
~~$13.00~~

5433
10" high
$14.00

971M
16" long
$16.00

971L
25" Long
$31.50

10.00

6418
23" high
$12.50

6632
16¼" high
$10.50

6921
Freeform
Approx.
14" dia.
7" high
$9.50

*6937
Approx.
22¼" high
~~$8.50~~

6841
21" high
$9.50

5

750

*629
8½″ high
$9.00

*629S
6″ high
$7.50

6925
7¾″ high
$7.50

6922
9½″ high
$8.00

*388
7½″ high
~~$7.00~~

*3744X
7″ dia.
$3.50

*6950
7¾″ high
$9.50

1100

800

850

*6839
14″ high
$7.00

*688
10″ high
$5.50

6823
14″ high
~~$10.50~~

*37
13″ high
$8.00

*49
10½″ high
~~$7.50~~

6027
17″ high
$10.50

*6516
14½″ high
~~$8.00~~

6

950

850

6948	6947	6949	6946	6924	6819	6812	6923
20½″ high	12″ high	12½″ high	10¾″ high	14″ high	13½″ high	9⅜″ high	16¼″ high
$9.00	$8.00	$8.00	$5.50	$8.00	$8.00	$4.00	$8.00

†675	†698	†697S	†697L
9¾″ dia.	9⅝″ dia.	8¼″ dia.	11½″ dia.
$3.50	$3.00	$2.50	$4.00

7
†696
13¼″ dia.
3¾″ high
$5.50
†684
7⅜″ dia.
$2.00
†696
13¼″ dia.
3¾″ high
$5.50
†6139
6¼″ dia.
$2.00
†684
7⅜″ dia.
$2.00
†69S
5⅝″ dia.
2″ high
$1.50
†69L
10¼″ dia.
4½″ high
$5.00
†695
10½″ dia.
$2.50
†624
9⅜″ dia
$3.00
†681
8⅛″ dia.
$2.50
†681
8⅛″ dia.
$2.50
†624
9⅜″ dia.
$3.00
†695
10½″ dia.
$2.50
†6143S
5½″ dia.
$1.50
†6143L
10½″ dia.
$5.00

8
6956
21″ high
$11.50
6942
11⅝″ high
$8.00
6953
21″ high
$13.50
Crystal Stopper with
Lemon or Tangerine
Bottle
6952
13″ high
$8.50
6810
10¾″ high
$6.00
6811
16¼″ high
$8.50
6955
22¾″ high
$16.00
6951
24″ high
$11.50
6954
27¼″ high
$13.00
6722
14″ high
$8.00
991
13½″ high
$8.00
6938
22½″ high
$8.50

9
900
1100
6933
15⅝″ high
~~$8.50~~
6934
20½″ high
~~$10.50~~
Crystal Stopper with
Lemon or Tangerine Bottle
6932
15″ high
$9.50
6930
12⅜″ high
$8.50
6936
18¾″ high
$9.00
6935
13½″ high
$8.50
900
900
6928
20¼″ high
~~$8.50~~
6927
15½″ high
$8.00
6929
20½″ high
$9.50
6941S
6½″ high
$5.50
6941L
10″ high
$7.00
6940
10″ high
$8.00
6939
18″ high
~~$8.50~~

10

6917
21¼″ high
~~$8.00~~

6914
8″ high
$5.00

6716
14¼″ high
~~$13.50~~
Crystal Stopper with
Lemon or Tangerine Bottle

6724
14″ high
$10.50
Crystal Stopper with
Lemon or Tangerine Bottle

6212
20½″ high
~~$10.50~~

†990A
3⅛″ dia.
$1.00

*990
12″ high
$8.00

6918
10⅝″ high
$5.50

6919
9½″ high
$6.00

6920
18½″ high
$9.00

6910
6¼″ high
$5.50

6916
6½″ high
$6.00

6915
11½″ high
$7.50

6931
Approx. 18″ high
$6.50

11
51L
Bubbles only
6″ dia.
$24.00 doz.
51M
Bubbles only
4½″ dia.
$15.60 doz.
51
Bubbles only
3″ dia.
$9.00 doz.
†691
3″ high
$1.00
†692
4⅜″ dia.
$1.00
†633
14″ long
$5.50
6943
7½″ high
$7.00
644
11″ high
$6.50
6320
3¼″ dia.
$6.00
6321
4¼″ dia.
$5.00
†666A
5½″ dia.
$1.50
666B
4½″ high
$4.00
6741
23¼″ high
$15.00
Crystal Stopper with
Lemon or Tangerine Bottle
†651F
9″ dia.
$4.00
†966
Approx.
8″ long
$2.00
†694
9½″—10″ dia.
$2.50
6736
22⅜″ high
$16.00
Crystal Stopper with
Lemon or Tangerine Bottle

Numbers with a reference mark (§) are available in the color combinations below.

CT — Crystal with turquoise trim
CO — Crystal with olive trim
CW — Crystal with wheat trim
TO — Turquoise with olive trim
LT — Lemon with tangerine trim
OT — Olive with turquoise trim

§*6830
14" high
15½" dia.
$27.50

§*6818
9" high
$6.50

§*6817-CT
9" high
$4.00

§*6817-CO
9" high
$4.00

§*6817-CW
9" high
$4.00

§*6817-TO
9" high
$4.00

§*6817-LT
9" high
$4.00

§*6817-OT
9" high
$4.00

§*6843
8½" high
$6.50

§*6838
15¾" high
$8.50

§*6840
6" high
15½" dia.
$11.50

§*6835
17½" high
$11.50

§*6831
23" high
$11.50

§*6834
17½" high
$9.50

13

*668S 6¼″ high $5.50

*6512 6″ high $6.00

*6726 9½″ high $9.00

*3750L 5½″ high $5.50

6511 9½″ high $6.00

*6714 9¾″ high $8.00

*418S 4½″ high $2.00

*418L 6″ high $2.00

6911 7½″ high $3.00

*636S 8″ high $6.00

6912 10″ high $6.00

*6944 9½″ high $6.00

*64B 13″ high $3.00

6945 6¾″ high $3.00

64D 11″ high $3.00

*6630S 8⅞″ high $6.50

6913 Approx. 11½″ high $3.00

*6424 5″ high $3.00

669 8½″ high $6.50

384 7½″ high $3.00

6926 Approx. 7″ high $16.00 pr.

†699A 6½″ high $6.50 pr.

†6813 7″ high $6.50 pr.

†6725 3½″ high 3¾″ wide $6.50 pr.

†699B 6½″ high $6.50 pr.

†434 5½″ high $6.50 pr.

14
†624
9⅜" dia.
$3.00
†681
8⅛" dia.
$2.50
†966
Assorted
8" long
$2.00
†675
9¾" dia.
$3.50
†684
7⅜" dia.
$2.00
†6139
6¼" dia.
$2.00
†698
9⅝" dia.
$3.00
†697L
11½" dia.
$4.00
†697S
8¼" dia.
$2.50
†666A
5½" dia.
$1.50
6321
4¼" dia.
$5.00
†693
7" dia.
$1.50
†651L
9" dia.
$4.00
†694
9½" dia.
$2.50
B508
6½" dia.
$6.50
59
Mixed Colors only
$1.00 box
472
$1.50 box

15
17⁵⁰
6138
Without Stopper
~~$16.00~~
6535
43″ high
$31.50
5815L
31″ high
$22.00
6534
29″ high
$26.50
6138W/S
35¾″ high
~~$18.50~~
20⁰⁰

16
†65J
8¼" dia.
$3.50
†65E
8¼" dia.
$3.50
†65B
8¼" dia.
$3.50
†65L
8¼" dia.
$3.50
†65F
8¼" dia.
$3.50
†65B
8¼" dia.
$3.50
†65K
8¼" dia.
$3.50
†65J
8¼" dia.
$3.50
68C
Approx.
3¾" dia.
$5.00
68D
Approx.
3¾" dia.
$5.00
68B
Approx.
3¾" dia.
$5.00
68E
Approx.
3¾" dia.
$5.00
68A
Approx.
3¾" dia.
$5.00

1970

1
TANGERINE
CRYSTAL
TURQUOISE
SURF GREEN
OLIVE GREEN
WHEAT
BLENKO COLORS 1970
† NUMBERS PRECEDED BY A DAGGER ARE NOT AVAILABLE IN TANGERINE.
EACH PIECE IS AVAILABLE IN ALL SIX COLORS, UNLESS MARKED OTHERWISE.
* NUMBERS PRECEDED BY AN ASTERISK ARE AVAILABLE IN CRACKLED AS WELL AS PLAIN FINISH.

2
7043L
14¾" high
$15.00
7043S
11¼" high
$13.00
7042
13" high
$16.00
7041
12" high
$13.00
7037
16½" high
$9.00
*7036
16⅞" high
$7.50
7017
7¼" high
$4.00
6937
Approx.
22¼" high
$10.00
*7012L
10" high
$7.00
*7015L
10" high
$8.50
*7012S
6⅞" high
$5.00
*7015S
7" high
$6.50
†990A
3⅛" dia.
$1.00
*990
12" high
$8.00
7048
19½" high
$18.00

3
6948
20½" high
$9.50
6947
12" high
$8.00
6949
12½" high
$8.00
7026
9⅞" high
$7.50
7027
9½" high
$8.00
7024
9⅝" high
$6.00
7025
9⁹⁄₁₆" high
$7.50
6819
13½" high
$8.00
6212
20½" high
$11.50
7045
12¼" high
$12.00
crystal with
colored trim
7046
10" high
$12.00
crystal with
colored trim
7044
14¾" high
$12.00
crystal with
colored trim
7038
13½" high
$10.00
crystal with
colored trim
6741
23¼" high
$15.00
crystal stopper with
tangerine bottle

4

†7040
15 7/16" dia.
$10.00

†7040
15 7/16" dia.
$10.00

†697L
11 1/2" dia.
$4.00

†624
9 3/8" dia.
$3.00

†695
10 1/2" dia.
$2.50

†698
9 5/8" dia.
$3.00

†697S
8 1/4" dia.
$2.50

5
†6143L
10½" dia.
$5.00
†6143S
5½" dia.
$1.50
†701
8½" dia.
$2.50
†675
9¾" dia.
$3.50
†703
10½" dia.
$5.00
†702
9¾" dia.
$4.00
†702
9¾" dia.
$4.00
†70
6¾" dia.
$2.00
†681
8⅛" dia.
$2.50

6
971L
25" long
$31.50
971M
16" long
$16.00
5433
10" high
$14.00
67S
15" high
6¾" dia. base
$13.50
crystal only
67L
17½" high
7" dia. base
$18.00
crystal only
6917
21¼" high
$8.50
6915
11½" high
$7.50
6918
10⅝" high
$5.50
7011
8⅜" high
$8.00
7010
6" high
$2.00
6914
8" high
$5.00
6916
6½" high
$6.00
6919
9½" high
$6.00

7
*629
8½" high
$9.00
*629S
6" high
$7.50
7034
8⅜" high
$8.00
*7035
8⅝" high
$8.50
6716
14¼" high
$14.50
crystal stopper with
tangerine bottle
6823
14" high
$11.00
7051
21⅝" high
$12.00
7039
6¼" high
$8.00
†633
14" long
$5.50
6923
16¼" high
$8.50

8
7029
16½″ high
$9.00
6953
21″ high
$14.50
crystal stopper with
tangerine bottle
7049
22″ high
$14.00
6810
10¾″ high
$6.00
6811
16¼″ high
$9.00
6952
13″ high
$10.00
6955
22¾″ high
$17.50
7032
9½″ high
$8.50
709
6¾″ high
$5.50
706
6¾″ high
$4.00
7031
9¾″ high
$8.00
6954
27¼″ high
$14.00

9
6934
20½" high
$11.00
crystal stopper with
tangerine bottle
6933
15⅝" high
$9.00
6956
21" high
$12.50
7033
16⅜" high
$10.00
6935
13½" high
$8.50
6938
22½" high
$9.00
6941L
10" high
$7.00
6941S
6½" high
$5.50
6939
18" high
$9.00
6942
11⅝" high
$8.00
6928
20¼" high
$9.00
991
13½" high
$8.00
6951
24" high
$12.50

10
6511 9½" high $6.00
7013 5½" high $6.00
*3750L 5½" high $5.50
6910 6¼" high $5.50
7014 6¾" high $6.50
*6714 9¾" high $8.00
*418S 4½" high $2.00
*418L 6" high $2.00
*6516 14½" high $8.50
*636S 8" high $6.00
669 8½" high $6.50
7019 11¾" high $7.50
7018 13⅜" high $6.50
6912 10" high $6.00
708 7 5/16" high $4.00
*6630S 8⅞" high $6.50
*6944 9½" high $6.00
6913 approx. 11½" high $3.00
64D 11" high $3.00
*64B 13" high $3.00
705 6⅛" high $3.00
*6424 5" high $3.00
6911 7½" high $3.00
704 6" high $3.00
6945 6¾" high $3.00
707 6⅛" high $4.00

11
51S
Bubbles only
3" dia.
$9.00 doz.
51L
Bubbles only
6" dia.
$24.00 doz.
51M
Bubbles only
4½" dia.
$15.60 doz.
*6840
6" high
15½" dia.
$11.50
*7028
5" high
11" dia.
$7.50
*6950
7¾" high
$9.50
*3744X
7" dia.
$3.50
*37
13" high
$8.00
*49
10½" high
$8.00
384
7½" high
$3.00
6812
9⅜" high
$4.00
*388
7½" high
$7.50
6321
4¼" dia.
$5.00
6320
3¼" dia.
$6.00
59
Mixed
Colors
Only
$1.00 box
472
$1.50 box
†699B
6½" high
$6.50 pr.
†699A
6½" high
$6.50 pr.
†6813
7" high
$6.50 pr.
†6725
3½" high
3¾" wide
$6.50 pr.
†434
5½" high
$6.50 pr.

12

†624
9⅜" dia.
$3.00

†681
8⅛" dia.
$2.50

†966
Assorted
8" long
$2.00

†693
7" dia.
$1.50

†694
9½" dia.
$2.50

†702
9¾" dia.
$4.00

†698
9⅝" dia.
$3.00

†697L
11½" dia.
$4.00

†697S
8¼" dia.
$2.50

†701
8½" dia.
$2.50

†651CN
9" dia.
$4.00

†675
9⅜" dia.
$3.50

†70
6¾" dia.
$2.00

†703
10½" dia.
$5.00

6321
4¼" dia.
$5.00

B508
6½" dia.
$6.50

13
Without Stopper
$17.50
6138W/S
35¾″ high
$20.00
7052
43½″ high
$35.00
7054
33″ high
$30.00
7053
36¼″ high
$30.00

14
7020L
Assorted colors
Approx. 3½" high
$5.00 ea.
7020M
Assorted colors
Approx. 3" high
$4.00 ea.
7020S
Assorted colors
Approx. 2½" high
$3.00 ea.
7020L
Assorted colors
Approx. 3½" high
$5.00 ea.
7020M
Assorted colors
Approx. 3" high
$4.00 ea.
7020S
Assorted colors
Approx. 2½" high
$3.00 ea.
Bienko Mushrooms are made entirely by hand; each one is unique. They are available in a multitude of color combinations.
7022S
8½" high
$6.00
7022M
11" high
$7.50
7022L
13½" high
$10.00
Mushroom stopper assortment
for 7022S-M-L Bottles

15

7016
9" high
crystal with colored hats
$6.00

7050
8½" Bottle height
crystal with colored
assorted stoppers
$10.00

7030
3½" high
Assorted colors
$27.00 per carton

Plastic egg holders pictured are **ADDITIONAL**

2" dia. x 1" High	$ .60
2" dia. x 1½" High	$ .70
2" dia. x 2" High	$ .80

Blenko Glass Eggs are made by hand. They are available in endless color combinations. Each egg is unique. Glass Eggs are available in packaged cartons of 6. The carton is a handsome package designed for maximum Point of Purchase impact.

Blenko Mushroom Clusters are handcrafted. Each cluster is unique. Available in crystal with assorted colored mushroom caps.

7047
11" high
Crystal/w/colored trim
$10.00

7021
6" high approx.
6" dia. base
$10.00

1971

BLENKO COLORS 1971

†† NUMBERS PRECEDED BY A DOUBLE DAGGER ARE NOT AVAILABLE IN TANGERINE OR CHARCOAL.
* NUMBERS PRECEDED BY AN ASTERISK ARE AVAILABLE IN CRACKLED AS WELL AS PLAIN FINISH.
EACH PIECE IS AVAILABLE IN ALL SIX COLORS, UNLESS MARKED OTHERWISE.
† NUMBERS PRECEDED BY A DAGGER ARE NOT AVAILABLE IN TANGERINE.
§ NUMBERS PRECEDED BY THIS SYMBOL ARE NOT AVAILABLE IN CHARCOAL.
ALL ITEMS MADE IN CHARCOAL WHICH HAVE HANDLES OR STEMS WILL HAVE THE HANDLES OR STEMS MADE OF CRYSTAL.

2
Disc
Disc
Disc
7043L
14¾" high
$15.00
7043S
11¼" high
$13.00
7112
14" high
$10.00
5.25
*7118
21½" high
$10.00
7120
12½" high
$8.00
7017
7¼" high
$4.50
*7036
16⅞" high
$8.00
*6937
22¼" high approx.
~~$10.00~~
5.25
Disc.
Disc
Disc
7127
13" high
$12.00
714
8½" high
$10.00
*7012S
6⅞" high
$5.00
*7015S
7" high
$6.50
††990A
3⅛" dia.
$1.00 ea.
*990
12" high
$8.00
Shade only
7048
19½" high
$18.00

3

*7111
12" high
$7.00

712L
9½" high
$7.00

712S
6½" high
$5.00

712M
8" high
$6.00

7027
9½" high
$8.00

7024
9⅝" high
$6.00

7025
9 9/16" high
$7.50

6819
13½" high
$8.00

6212
20½" high
$12.00

7119W/S
18" high
$12.00
~~Crystal stopper with~~
tangerine bottle

7119
14½" high
$8.00

7114
16½" high
$12.00

*7126
14" high
$10.00

6741
23¼" high
~~$15.00~~
Crystal stopper with
tangerine bottle

6

Disc

971L
22"
$31.50

971M
16" long
$16.00

5433
10" high
$14.00

675
15" high
6¾" dia. at base
$14.00
crystal only

7177
8½" high
punch bowl
$9.00

Disc

Disc

6918
10⅝" high
$5.50

6915
11½" high
$8.00

*719
17" high
$8.00

*7121
10½" high
$8.50

715
8" high
$6.00

6914
8" high
$5.00

6916
6½" high
$6.50

6919
9½" high
$6.50

7

Disc Disc

*629
8½" high
$9.00

*629S
6" high
$7.50

7034
8⅜" high
$8.50

*7035
8⅝" high
$8.50

6716
14¼" high
~~$15.00~~ 16.00
crystal stopper with
tangerine bottle

8.00

Disc

Lamp 26.00
Shade 6.00
32 inches
25 lbs

Disc

7110
18½" high
$14.00

7051
21⅝" high
~~$12.50~~
6.50

7039
6¼" high
$8.50

†1633
14" long
$6.00

6923
16¼" high
$8.50

8

7029	6953	7049	6810	6811	6952
16½" high	21" high	22" high	10¾" high	16¼" high	13" high
~~$9.00~~ 4.75	$15.00	$15.00	$6.00	$9.00	~~$10.00~~ 5.25
	crystal stopper with tangerine bottle				

6955	7032	709	706	7031	6954
22¾" high	9½" high	6¾" high	6¾" high	9¾" high	27¼" high
~~$17.50~~ 9.00	$8.50	$5.50	$4.00	$8.00	$15.00

9

27 inches
Lamp 22.50
13 lbs
Shade 4.00

Disc

Lamp
17.00
Shade
3.00
21½ inches
17.00
12 lbs

Disc

6934
20½" high
$12.00
crystal stopper with
tangerine bottle

7124S
6½" high
$5.00

7124L
12½" high
$7.00

7124M
9½" high
$6.00

6956
21" high
$13.50

7033
16⅜" high
$10.00

*7139
6½" high
$5.00

6935
13½" high
$8.50

23 inches
Lamp
$17.50
Shade
3.00
12 lbs.

Disc

Lamp
$23.50
Shade
4.00
16 lbs
28 inches

*7166L
13" high
$7.50

*7166M
10" high
$6.00

6939
18" high
$9.00

6942
11⅝"
$8.00

6928
20¼" high
$10.00

991
13½" high
$8.00

6951
24" high
$13.50

10
Disc
Disc
Disc
6511
9½" high
$6.00
*7113
8½" high
$8.50
*3750L
5½" high
$5.50
6910
6¼" high
$5.50
7014
6¾" high
$6.50
*6714
9¾" high
$8.50
*418S
4½" high
$2.00
*418L
6" high
$2.00
Disc
Disc
Disc
*6516
14½" high
$8.50
*636S
8" high
$6.00
717
15" high
$7.50
7019
11¾" high
$7.50
7018
13⅜" high
$7.00
6912
10" high
$6.00
*7141
9" high
$5.50
*718
14" high
$7.50
*6944
9½" high
$6.50
Disc
7123
11" high
$8.00
64D
11" high
$3.00
*64B
11" high
$3.00
*705
6⅛" high
$3.00
*708
7 5/16" high
$4.00
*6424
5" high
$3.00
704
6" high
$3.00
*7117
8" high
$6.50
*713
10½" high
$4.50
707
6⅛" high
$4.00

11
51S
bubbles only
3" dia.
$9.00 doz.
51L
bubbles only
6" dia.
$24.00 doz.
51M
bubbles only
4½" dia.
$15.60 doz.
*6840
6" high
15½" dia.
$12.00
*7028
5" high
11" dia.
$7.50
*6950
7¾" high
$10.00
*3744X
7" dia.
$4.00
*37
13" high
$8.00
*49
10½" high
$8.00
384
7½" high
$3.50
6812
9⅜" high
$4.00
*388
7½" high
$7.50
6321
4¼" dia.
$5.00
6320
3¼" dia.
$6.00
59
mixed colors
only
$1.00 box
§472
$1.50 box
††699B
6½" high
$6.50 pr.
††699A
6½" high
$6.50 pr.
††6813
7" high
$6.50 pr.
††6725
3½" high
3¾" wide
$6.50 pr.
††434
5½" high
$6.50 pr.

14
*7144
11" dia.
$10.00
*7143S
6½" high
$5.00
*7143L
12½" high
$7.50
*7143M
8½" high
$6.00
7125
14½" high
$12.00
*7137
10½" dia.
$6.00
*7128S
8" high
$8.00
*7128L
10" high
$10.00
716
9½" high
$7.50
7122
9½" high
$15.00
*7115S
5½" high
$5.00
7115M
6½" high
$6.00
*7115L
8" high
$7.00
*7116
6½" high
$7.50

15
Blenko mushrooms are made entirely by hand; each one is unique. They are available in a multitude of color combinations.
§7020L
assorted colors
approx. 3½" high
$5.00 each
§7020M
assorted colors
approx. 3" high
$4.00 each
§7020S
assorted colors
approx. 2½" high
$3.00 each
§711F
approx. 6" high
$7.50
§711D
approx. 6" high
$7.50
§711B
approx. 6" high
$7.50
§711E
approx. 6" high
$7.50
§711C
approx. 6" high
$7.50
§711A
approx. 6" high
$7.50

Ship all these lamps by Freight
13
Lamp
29.00
Shade $6.00
without stopper
$17.50
42½ inches
Lamp
37.00
Shade
$6.00
45 inches
Lamp
$34.00
Shade $6.00
38 inches
Lamp
$34.00
Shade
$6.00
41½
Disc
Disc
6138W/S
35¾" high
$20.00
7052
43½" high
$35.00
7054
33" high
$30.00
7053
36¼" high
$30.00

16

†65CP
8¼" dia.
$3.50

†65LE
8¼" dia.
$3.50

†65PS
8¼" dia.
$3.50

†65SG
8¼" dia.
$3.50

†65GM
8¼" dia.
$3.50

†65SC
8¼" dia.
$3.50

†65CN
8¼" dia.
$3.50

†65AQ
8¼" dia.
$3.50

†65TR
8¼" dia.
$3.50

†65VR
8¼" dia.
$3.50

†65AR
8¼" dia.
$3.50

†65LB
8¼" dia.
$3.50

†68D
approx. 3¾" dia.
$5.00

68C
approx. 3¾" dia.
$5.00

†68E
approx. 3¾" dia.
$5.00

†68B
approx. 3¾" dia.
$5.00

†68A
approx. 3¾" dia.
$5.00

§68F
approx. 3¾" dia.
$5.00

§68F
approx. 3¾" dia.
$5.00

1972-1999 Covers

BLENKO 76

BLENKO 77

BLENKO 78

BLENKO 79

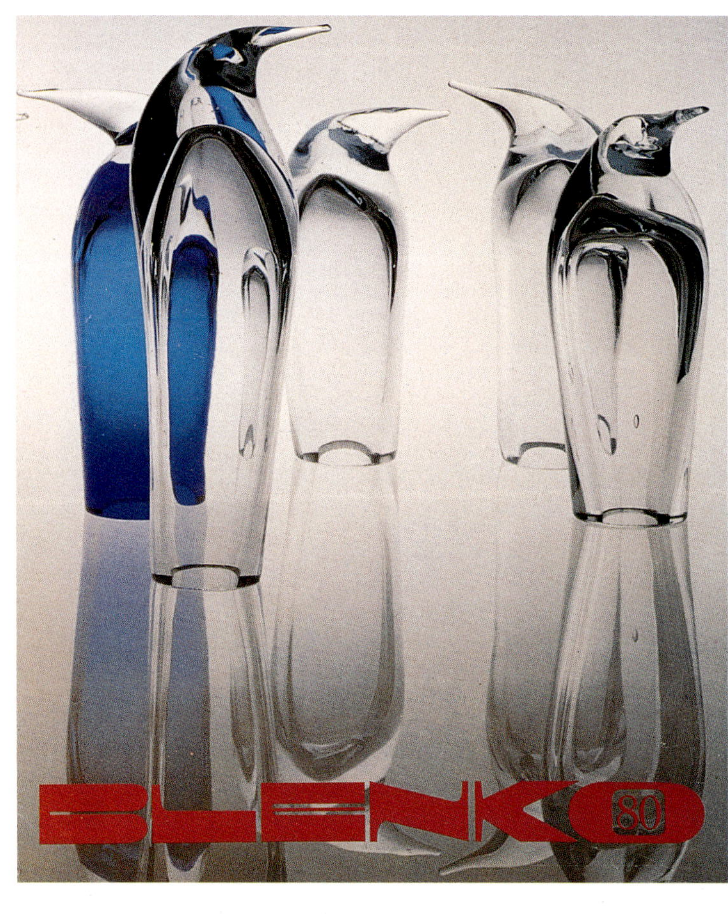
BLENKO 80

BLENKO 81

BLENKO 82

BLENKO 83

84
BLENKO 84

85
BLENKO 85

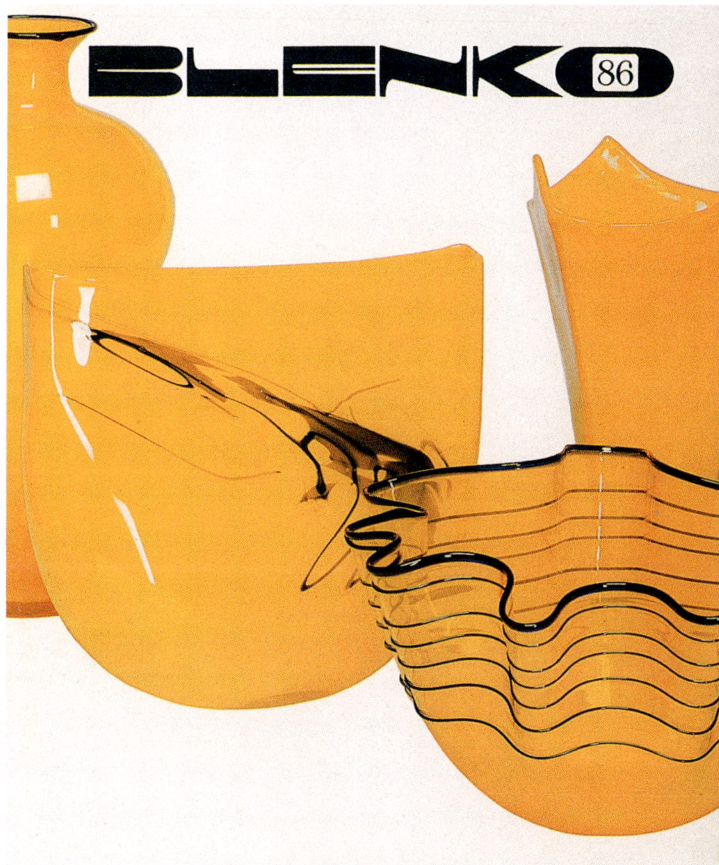
BLENKO 86

BLENKO 87

BLENKO 88

BLENKO 89

BLENKO
1990

BLENKO
1991

BLENKO 1992

BLENKO 1993

BLENKO
PROOF COPY
RETAIL

BLENKO

BlEnKo 96

BLENKO 97
Hand Blown Glass Catalog

BLENKO 98

BLENKO 99

Price Guide

The first two digits signify the date of introduction (90s indicate early 1950s). The last digit(s) indicate the design order in that year. Price amounts are in U.S. dollars and for single items, even if they are shown in pairs.

(Abbreviations:S=small; M=medium; L=large; LL=extra large; P=pitcher; SL=small leaf; ML=medium leaf; LL=large leaf; DOF=double old fashioned; w/s=with stopper; C=crackle)

Item	Price
361P	$35-45
366M	$40-50
366L	$50-60
366SL	$50-60
366ML	$70-80
366LL	$90-110
37	$50-60
3716	$30-40
3744X	$30-40
3750L	$30-40
384	$20-30
388	$40-50
404S	$30-40
404M	$40-50
413L	$50-60
418S	$15-20
418L	$15-20
418DOF	$20-25
434	$10-15
452	$20-30
489	$60-80
49	$50-60
508	$20-30
51S	$5-10
51L	$10-20
533	$20-30
537	$30-40
538	$30-40
5318	$20-30
546	$50-60
5433	$75-100
555	$25-35
5516w/s	$150-175
5519M	$35-45
5519L	$55-65
569P	$50-60
5616B	$40-50
5616C	$55-65
588	$175-225
5815S	$75-100
5815M	$125-150
5815L	$200-250
5825S	$100-125
5929L	$200-250
C60A	$15-20
C60B	$15-20
C60C	$15-20
C60D	$15-20
C60E	$15-20
C60F	$15-20
603	$25-35
607	$40-50
6023	$20-30
6027	$100-125
6029	$150-175
6030S	$25-35
6030M	$45-55
6030L	$65-75
6037	$100-125
6041	$60-70
6042P	$50-60
6046	$40-50
611S	$25-35
619	$30-40
6110	$50-60
6112S	$15-20
6112L	$25-25
6113	$60-70
6115S	$40-50
6115M	$60-80
6115L	$100-125
6117	$60-80
6118	$25-35
6120	$45-55
6122S	$75-100
6122M	$100-125
6122L	$150-200
6123S	$40-50
6123M	$50-60
6123L	$75-100
6123LL	$175-225
6124	$25-35
6128	$10-15
6137	$100-125
6138w/s	$200-225
6139	$15-20
6141	$20-30
6143S	$10-15
6143M	$20-25
6143L	$30-40
6147	$50-60
6148	$35-45
621S	$25-35
621M	$35-45
621L	$45-55
622S	$30-40
622M	$40-50
622L	$60-70
623S	$30-40
623L	$45-55
624	$15-20
625S	$10-15
625M	$20-25
625L	$30-40
626S	$60-70
626M	$100-125
626L	$125-175
627S	$50-60
627L	$75-100
627LL	$175-225
628S	$100-125
628L	$175-225
629S	$25-35

629M	$35-45
629L	$55-65
6210	$75-100
6211	$100-125
6212S	$75-100
6212M	$100-125
6212	$150-200
6213	$100-125
6214	$75-100
6215	$75-100
6216	$75-100
6217	$75-100
6218	$120-140
6219S	$25-35
6219L	$35-45
6220S	$40-50
6220L	$60-70
6221	$50-60
6222	$30-40
6223	$50-60
6224S	$40-50
6224L	$70-80
6225S	$75-100
6225L	$100-125
6226	$50-60
6227	$50-60
6228	$125-150
6229	$90-110
6230	$100-125
6231	$150-200
63A1	$10-15
63A2	$15-20
63B1	$15-20
63B2	$15-20
63B3	$20-25
631S	$10-15
631L	$20-25
632	$15-20
633	$35-45
634	$30-40
635	$30-40
636S	$45-55
636L	$65-85
637S	$20-25
637M	$30-35
637L	$40-45
638S	$60-70
638M	$75-100
638L	$125-150
639	$75-100
6310	$75-100
6311S	$60-80
6311M	$80-100
6311L	$125-150
6312S	$25-35
6312M	$35-45
6312L	$50-60
6313S	$40-50
6313L	$50-60
6314	$150-175
6315	$125-150
6316	$150-200
6317	$40-50
6318	$35-45
6319	$15-20
6320	$20-25
6321	$20-25
6322	$30-40
6323S	$25-35
6323M	$35-45
6323L	$55-65
6326	$10-15
64A	$25-35
64B	$25-35
64C	$20-30
64D	$25-35
64E	$25-30
641S	$15-20
641L	$30-40
642S	$15-20
642L	$15-20
643	$25-35
644	$30-40
645	$40-50
646	$75-100
647	$90-110
648	$100-125
649	$75-100
6410	$35-45
6411	$15-20
6412	$30-40
6413	$70-90
6414	$40-50
6415	$70-90
6416	$70-90
6417	$75-100
6418	$100-150
6419	$35-45
6420	$50-70
6421	$50-70
6422	$70-90
6423	$125-150
6424	$25-35
6425	$125-150
6426	$100-150
6427	$100-150
6428	$25-35
65	$15-20
650	$10-15
651	$15-25
652	$20-25
653	$65-85
654	$65-85
655	$20-25
656S	$30-40
656M	$50-60
656L	$70-90
657S	$60-80
657M	$70-90
657L	$100-125
657LL	$150-200
658S	$60-70
658L	$75-100
659S	$30-40
659L	$60-70
6510	$55-65
6511	$30-40
6512	$25-35
6513	$35-45
6514	$50-70
6515	$60-70
6516	$75-100
6517	$45-55
6518	$40-50
6519	$60-70
6520	$70-80
6521	$100-125
6522	$20-25
6523	$40-50
6524S	$50-60
6524L	$70-80
6525	$100-150
6526	$75-100
6527	$100-150
6528S	$100-125
6528L	$175-225
6529	$125-175
6530S	$70-90
6530L	$90-110
6531	$60-80
6532	$75-100
6533	$100-125
6534	$200-250
6535	$200-250
6536	$100-150
661	$10-15
662	$10-15
663	$20-25
664	$20-30
665A	$10-15
665B	$10-15
665C	$10-15
666A	$10-15
666B	$10-15
667S	$20-25
667L	$30-40
668S	$25-35
668L	$35-45

669	$50-60
6610	$30-40
6611	$65-85
6612	$25-35
6613	$50-60
6614	$30-40
6615S	$60-70
6615L	$75-100
6616	$35-45
6617	$60-70
6618	$60-80
6619	$40-50
6620	$25-35
6621	$30-40
6622	$40-50
6623	$60-70
6624S	$25-35
6624L	$35-45
6625	$50-60
6626S	$75-100
6626L	$100-125
6627	$90-110
6628	$70-90
6629	$75-100
6630S	$40-50
6630L	$75-100
6631	$125-150
6632	$70-90
6633	$65-75
6634	$75-100
67S	$40-50
67L	$50-60
672	$25-35
675	$20-25
677	$40-50
678	$60-75
679	$40-50
6710A	$70-90
6710B	$70-90
6711S	$100-125
6711L	$125-150
6712	$1001-25
6713	$175-225
6714	$35-45
6715	$100-125
6716	$125-150
6717	$125-175
6718	$25-35
6719	$35-45
6720	$35-45
6721S	$50-60
6721L	$70-80
6722	$50-60
6723	$50-60
6724	$75-100
6725	$15-25
6726	$35-45
6727	$50-60
6728	$80-100
6729	$25-35
6730	$25-30
6731	$50-60
6732S	$125-150
6732L	$150-200
6733	$50-60
6734	$70-90
6735	$65-75
6736	$125-150
6737	$75-100
6738	$125-150
6739	$175-225
6740	$60-80
6741	$150-175
6742	$50-70
6743	$70-90
6744	$60-70
6745	$150-200
6746	$125-150
6747	$100-125
68A	$30-40
68B	$30-40
68C	$30-40
68D	$30-40
68E	$30-40
68F	$30-40
681	$15-20
683	$10-15
684	$10-15
685S	$10-15
685L	$20-30
686	$20-30
687	$30-40
688	$40-50
689	$35-45
6810	$40-50
6811	$70-90
6812	$40-50
6813	$15-20
6814	$70-90
6815	$70-90
6816	$90-110
6817	$70-90
6818	$70-90
6819	$70-90
6820	$75-100
6821	$75-100
6822	$125-150
6823	$70-90
6824	$40-60
6825	$40-50
6826A	$30-40
6826B	$30-40
6827	$70-90
6828	$70-90
6829	$75-100
6830	$100-150
6831	$125-150
6832	$60-70
6833	$35-45
6834	$100-125
6835	$125-150
6836	$75-100
6837	$60-70
6838	$100-125
6839	$60-70
6840	$60-80
6841	$70-90
6842	$100-125
6843	$60-70
69S	$10-15
69L	$25-35
691	$10-15
692	$10-15
693	$10-15
694	$15-20
695	$15-20
696	$25-35
697S	$20-25
697L	$25-35
698	$20-30
699A	$15-20
699B	$15-20
6910	$20-25
6911	$20-25
6912	$60-80
6913	$25-35
6914	$25-35
6915	$60-70
6916	$30-40
6917	$100-125
6918	$30-40
6919	$30-40
6920	$100-125
6921	$50-60
6922	$35-45
6923	$60-80
6924	$70-90
6925	$25-35
6926	$15-25
6927	$60-70
6928	$75-100
6929	$70-90
6930	$50-60
6931	$60-70
6932	$60-70
6933	$60-70
6934	$125-150
6935	$70-90

6936	$100-125
6937	$90-110
6938	$100-150
6939	$100-125
6940	$30-40
6941S	$25-35
6941L	$40-50
6942	$70-90
6943	$20-25
6944	$65-75
6945	$20-25
6946	$40-50
6947	$60-80
6948	$100-125
6949	$50-60
6950	$30-40
6951	$125-175
6952	$50-60
6953	$125-175
6954	$150-175
6955	$125-150
6956	$70-90
70	$10-15
701	$20-25
702	$20-25
703	$20-25
704	$20-25
705	$20-25
706	$15-20
707	$20-25
708	$40-50
709	$20-30
7010	$10-15
7011	$25-35
7012S	$20-30
7012L	$30-40
7013	$20-25
7014	$20-25
7015S	$25-35
7015L	$35-45
7016	$75-100
7017	$20-25
7018	$70-90
7019	$70-90
7020S	$10-15
7020M	$15-20
7020L	$20-25
7021	$30-40
7022S	$50-60
7022M	$70-80
7022L	$90-120
7024	$35-45
7025	$25-35
7026	$25-30
7027	$25-30
7028	$25-35
7029	$60-70
7030	$15-25
7031	$25-35
7032	$30-40
7033	$60-70
7034	$25-35
7035	$25-35
7036	$100-125
7037	$125-150
7038	$80-100
7039	$30-40
7040	$35-45
7041	$90-100
7042	$100-125
7043S	$100-125
7034L	$125-150
7044	$100-125
7045	$100-125
7046	$100-125
7047	$125-150
7048	$70-90
7049	$80-100
7050	$100-125
7051	$70-90
7052	$200-250
7053	$175-225
7054	$175-225
71A	$25-35
71B	$25-35
71C	$25-35
71D	$25-35
71E	$25-35
71F	$25-35
712S	$20-25
712M	$25-30
712L	$30-35
713	$40-50
714	$25-35
715	$40-50
716	$40-50
717	$70-90
718	$75-100
719	$75-100
7110	$60-70
7111	$40-50
7112	$50-60
7113	$30-40
7114	$50-60
7115S	$20-25
7115M	$30-35
7115L	$40-45
7116	$30-40
7117	$30-40
7118	$100-150
7119	$60-70
7119w/s	$75-100
7120	$40-50
7121	$50-60
7122	$50-60
7123	$55-65
7125	$60-80
7126	$60-80
7127	$100-125
7128S	$25-30
7128L	$40-50
7137	$25-35
7139	$25-35
7141	$35-45
7143S	$30-40
7143M	$40-50
7143L	$60-70
7144	$35-45
7166M	$40-50
7166L	$50-60
7177	$40-50
920S	$30-40
920M	$60-80
920L	$100-125
939P	$60-70
955L	$50-60
964S	$75-100
964L	$125-150
966	$20-30
971S	$50-60
971M	$70-80
971L	$100-125
976	$75-100
990	$40-50
990A	$10-15
991	$55-65
993	$20-30